Birthing Samuel

Birthing Samuel

Releasing Yesterday's Pain—
Embracing Tomorrow's Potential

Stephanie W. Gant

To order additional copies of this book, contact:
Xlibris Corporation
1-888-795-4274
www.Xlibris.com
Orders@Xlibris.com
43087

CONTENTS

This book is dedicated to

Mom and Cassandra—
Women of great strength and courage

Introduction

Most days I can be found wearing a pretty warm smile. Of course, if anyone has reason to smile certainly I do. Just to think, God has called me into a place of intimacy in Him, a place where I clearly hear His voice and sense the realness of His touch. For this awesome privilege, I wear a smile. Then there's my husband: I believe him to be the kindest, most gentle man in all of God's creation. Even after twenty-three years of marriage, just thinking of him sets my entire countenance aglow. And there is no way I can leave out my four children. They continuously make me so proud. My three daughters are all grown up, and just observing as they each seek for their individual spiritual places is yet another reason behind my smile. My son, who is the youngest, also has a heart for God. Although he is only sixteen, I clearly can see his spiritual form taking shape. Indeed, God has richly blessed my life, so smiling just seems to come natural. However, in all fairness, I have to let you in on a little secret . . . . *It hasn't always been this way.*

Quite the opposite of the glorious life I just described, I went through a season where I was so broken and shattered. It was as if the bottom had fallen out of everything. The impact of my many youthful bad decisions, as well as the ones related to my stubborn and rebellious attitude, finally caught up with me; and, with no real warning, everything, my whole life, began to crash. When the thick cloud of dust finally began to settle, I was still standing all right, but I had been robbed and stripped totally of all that brought value. All that it takes to make a woman feel good about herself—it was all gone! I felt I had no value; I felt I had no worth. Peering at my own reflection,

I appeared small and insignificant. Hidden darkness, hidden scars, emotional wounds, as well as a few generational demons—they all were holding me captive in a place where I really had no desire to be. Yet I felt absolutely powerless to break free. Thinking back, I distinctly remember feeling that I was nothing more than hollow flesh. In vain I searched and searched, in all the wrong places, trying to fill the deep emptiness that seemed to have no end.

For the deep, deep barrenness that daily echoed throughout my inner most self, I wept. For that same all too familiar barrenness that I now see in many of you because your value and worth have been stripped away, I weep. I weep because I know what a frightening, dark place it is. I weep because I know it's often difficult and confusing as you attempt to tunnel your way out. I weep because I know how hard it is just to muster the strength to keep going and not give up. I weep because I know that if you will just hold on, in due time, God will minister healing to all of the broken places in your life. He will restore your sense of value and worth and make it possible for you to hold your head up high as you take your rightful place.

I can't help but be touched and moved with compassion as I meet those who are suffering with self-esteem issues. Many have lost sight of all the many abilities, talents, and potentials that God has placed deep within them. Once upon a time maybe they did dare to dream. Perhaps they dreamed of accomplishing great feats, building successful careers, or just living out their idea of the great American dream. Then one unsuspecting day that started out pretty routinely, at some point during that twenty-four hour period, something happened, something catastrophic. And from that day forward, nothing was ever the same again.

Please really hear and digest the following statements: When others fail to see and to affirm your value, it is tragic and most unfortunate. However, through your own eyes, when you fail to see your great value and worth, that is nothing short of emotional suicide. Although physically alive, emotionally you have shut down. Please, I beg that you must not buy into the enemy's lies as he tells you that you have no real purpose upon the earth, nothing significant to give. Refuse to accept as he tells you that even if your life ceased no one would notice. It is his job to keep you in your current state of hopeless despair. He loves it when you feel that nothing is ever going to work out in your favor. Oh, how he enjoys watching as you sink deeper and deeper into that cruel, black hole of depression. If this happens to be where you are, if this is the reality of the world where you reside, then this book was written just for you.

Returning home after pouring out my heart at a conference, you cannot even begin to imagine, nor can I adequately articulate, the pain that I feel knowing that I left behind many who still are so broken. I never really thought about it before, but what I feel must be pretty similar to what a doctor experiences when he just can't seem to cut away all the cancer. He leaves that operating table fully aware that the disease is going to continue to spread and fester. He knows that death is inevitable; it's just a matter of time.

As I make direct eye contact with my audience, I can't help but notice the deep, deep creases across many foreheads; the long, pensive stares into seemingly nowhere; and the elongated, sunken cheeks. I feel the inner sadness and turmoil as the solemn faces communicate that all sense of self-worth and self-esteem deserted long ago. At that point, it's almost as if I'm somehow caught up in a vicarious moment: Within me I literally will begin to feel their hurts, and I feel their burdens as they are seemingly transferred upon my shoulders. For a few minutes there I am; I cannot escape the pain. I can only hope that while in the midst of that experience, God will grant that I be allowed to help shoulder some of the burden so that those who are suffering might be granted at least a measure of relief from its full weight.

Some who are suffering self-esteem issues don't have a history of what we would consider to be severe abuse, but their pain is still very real. Perhaps their emotional wounding began in elementary school as the children teased and taunted them concerning weight, hair, or clothing. I know this has to take your mind back to your school days. After all these years, I still can remember vividly those who were the outcasts. I remember the children poking fun at those who, for reasons beyond their own control, were reduced to wearing dirty clothing and who had unpleasant body odors. Children can be so cruel to each other, and the impact often results in lifetime hurts. As moms and dads, we absolutely must teach our children to respect emotions. Even as they play and joke with their peers, there are certain emotional boundaries that never should be crossed. Just as they are taught the importance of keeping their hands to themselves, they must also be taught concerning the dangers of their little mouths. Contrary to what you and I were told, words do hurt and saying you're sorry does not always stop the hurt. There are times when being sorry is just not enough.

I acknowledge that some emotional pains are more traumatizing than others. However, it is not my intent to make judgment on the severity of individual cases. We are all different. An experience that one may undergo causing minimal emotional damage may very well bring total devastation to another. My focus throughout this book is very singular: It is simply to convince you that whatever life's experiences may have stripped from you, they did not strip away nor did they alter God's divine purpose for your life. God has preserved you for your purpose, and He has preserved your purpose for you. It is still there waiting for you! No matter how you feel, no matter what you may think, and no matter what you may have been told throughout your life, you are a person of extraordinary value and worth.

Some of the stories that I am going to share are on the light side. They are meant to make you smile as you reflect upon similar experiences. Then there are other pages . . . . As you read them, perhaps you will feel a tear or two flowing as you are brought face to face with your current realities. From beginning to end, there is only one underlying theme—God's great love and concern for you. You are forefront on His mind. He hurts because you're hurting. He pains as He observes you walking with your head hung down, refusing to look up, refusing to speak up, all because you feel that *you* have no value and nothing of worth to contribute. Notice here that the emphasis is on *you*. What someone else thinks of you is not the problem. The real issue at hand is what you think of yourself.

As you turn each page, you must see yourself stepping out of those old bondages. Feel as those old, heavy, rusty chains break and hear them as they clang upon the cold, lifeless cement of your past. If you dare to keep reading (*please, please keep reading*), you will be introduced to one of God's most prized creations. This person is obviously very special to God because He took great care to place within her such unique gifts and abilities. As you continue reading a little more . . . and then a little more . . . hopefully soon you will discover that the prized creation with such a vast storehouse of buried treasure within is "YOU!"

Chapter One

Through Another's Eyes

The very realness of our need for affirmation can be seen clearly through many of our everyday experiences. How many times have I tried a new hairstyle and just couldn't make up my mind? Did I like it or not? What should have been a rather uncomplicated yes or no decision somehow became a serious, long, drawn out dilemma filled with way too much anxiety. It usually wasn't until my husband, children, and a few others positively complimented me that I finally found the confidence to say, "Yes! I really do like this style on me. I wish I had gotten it a lot sooner." I don't even have to ask if you can identify. I know that you can. Whether it's our hair, an outfit, or some random project that we are working on, we need to be affirmed. I know you have met that special group of people who claim that they absolutely don't care what anyone else says or thinks about them. Well, they can continue to deceive themselves if they so desire, but you and I know the truth. We all are dependent upon each other, physically as well as emotionally. It is not by accident that we are this way. It is purely by design—God's design.

I often think back upon an encounter I had with a group of young people standing outside my church one Sunday. Although I have long forgotten the exact nature of our conversation, there was this one young man who made a simple yet pretty profound declaration. After a bunch of teasing and horseplay back and forth, I finally looked at that young man and asked what he had to contribute to the conversation. Jokingly he looked at me and said, "I don't know right now, but I will have something to bring to the table." WOW! In his own special way, he was saying, *Don't count me out. I am valuable, and I have something of worth to contribute.* We can all identify with wanting to believe that what we contributed to a conversation would be accepted and not viewed as foolish or insignificant. How about all of those times in school when we were hesitant to ask a question or to make a statement? Do you remember the cautious way that we approached answering a question that was already on the floor? Sure you do. Our hesitancies about speaking out were grounded in the fact that we did not want to suffer humiliation in front of our classmates. We did not want to say or do anything that would cause them in any way to devalue our worth.

Before we proceed further, I have developed a practical exercise that will nicely set the stage for the discussion that follows. Take time to meditate on the questions being asked. Carefully think through your responses.

Exercise:

With 1 being the least and 10 being the greatest, how would you rate your overall value as a person?

As you pondered the question, what factors had the greatest influence on your self-rating?

Without benefit of your responses to the above exercise, I feel safe in saying that your self-rating was probably greatly impacted by how you perceive that you measure up in the eyes of others. Self-value is not a sole matter of what we think of ourselves. It is largely our perception of what others think, feel, and say about us. If we live in an environment where we are highly praised and consistently affirmed, we tend to develop a higher self-view. However, when we are always met with brow-beating and criticism and are made to feel that nothing we do is ever quite good enough, certainly those experiences have a very negative impact and our self-esteem greatly suffers. That is why we must be extra cautious and carefully screen those persons whom we allow to become a part of our inner circle. Once inside your inner circle, whether positively or negatively, building up or tearing down, they are absolutely going to speak into your life, and your self-value will be impacted by their words. Sometimes, as is the case with family, we are not afforded the opportunity to select those persons who are born into or who will marry into our circle. However, when there is clearly a choice of selection to be made and the decision is fully in our hands, we need to proceed with caution. Never blindly pull people into an intimate place beside you. Once inside that intimate place, they will have the power to influence your thinking, even your thoughts concerning yourself.

You must know into whose hands you are entrusting your emotions. If you are entrusting them into the hands of one who has severe emotional wounds, the impact upon your own self-esteem is bound to be devastating. Why? As just stated, that person is going to speak into your life, and you will be greatly impacted by the words spoken. Let me share a personal observation concerning my own life. Hopefully it will bring a degree of clarity to the message that I am trying to relay. I know that you will be able to identify.

I am a wife, a mom, the first lady of my church, the church administrator, women's department coordinator, and every other coordinator that no-one else will step to the plate and be. And, as if all of that isn't enough, I also am engaged actively in my own full-time ministry. Sometimes the stress level is on overload, and I lack the ability to articulate my emotions as they short fuse and go haywire. During those times when my emotions are literally bouncing all over the place, I definitely have heard myself responding to others with a certain impersonal coolness. I also have noticed (with later regret) the sort of callous and not well thought through statements that somehow just seem to flow from my mouth. Because I now am so aware, I try to be extra cautious during those high stress times. It's important to me that I don't wound or make anyone feel small. I want people to know that I value them, and I value what they have to say. I have dedicated my life to the ministry of healing; heaven forbid that I should wound.

Now this is the point: When people are hurting, they really do hurt other people. If there are those in your life who constantly demean and attack your value, chances are it is because they themselves lack self-value. Those who live with the ravages of emotional pain are more likely to inflict pain. And generally, that pain is released upon those closest to them. Unfortunately, the only way that some can feel good about themselves is by tearing others down. Yet in all fairness, we must acknowledge that everyone who is guilty of abusive behavior is not necessarily cruel and unfeeling. However, many simply are acting out of their pain, a pain so phenomenal and so never ending that it literally spills over into all that they say and do. And as much as they inwardly might desire otherwise, never are they free from the influences of their pain.

It is a huge mistake for you not to consider that just as you are hurting, there are many others who also are suffering from emotional wounding. All too well they know the cruel pangs of rejection, and its effect on their self-value and self-worth has been devastating. I am really not sure exactly where we got off course as a society, but no one can deny that there is an overwhelming flood of those who are coming forward with such debilitating emotional issues. In fact, their issues are so debilitating that these individuals often cannot function in any organized system. The schools, workforce, and our communities all bear witness to this truth. Just observe the myriad problems in the school systems (such as gang activity, drop-out rate, uncontrollable behavior, and violence), beginning in the elementary grades all the way through the college level. Our communities are also filled with young men and young women who just can't seem to maintain a job. Indeed, by anyone's definition, we have a full-fledged epidemic on our hands.

I was speaking with a young lady who is in the midst of trying to regain a sense of value after what seems to have been a lifetime of abuse. The interesting thing about her is that she comes from somewhat of an elitist background. No one would have ever dared imagine what everyday life was like behind the walls of her world. In the minds of the masses, certain behaviors and problems are often limited to certain neighborhoods or to certain groups of people. However, the truth is that every ugly, debasing form of abuse can be found in everyone's neighborhood. It crosses every line and every barrier—social, economic, racial, and gender. And those who have been abuse victims seem to share a few common traits. Generally, they are all left with an inward need to search out and lay claim to their true identities as well as find some sense of self-value.

The Awakening

At some point in life, most people come to a place of awakening. I truly believe that I myself am in the midst of such a season. It is a place where you lose tolerance for everything in your life that is not real and that is not of a genuine nature. You want truth revealed, even the truth of exactly who you are and what you were meant to accomplish. Refusing to hide behind any more masks, one by one you face your issues and all of the deep-rooted pain that has controlled you over the years. You acknowledge that your emotional wounds have greatly influenced and shaped the person that you have become, but you also acknowledge that possibly there is another person—one whom you may have never met—who has been buried beneath all the hurts. You want to meet that person. Who is she? What is she capable of accomplishing apart from all the pain and the wounding? If you find that you are also in the awakening season of your life, don't be afraid to uncover that which has been concealed. For every new discovery that can add to the person you are—embrace and cherish it. It is a genuine part of your identity. Proudly adorn yourself with your new treasured find and walk into the fullness of who you were created to be.

Let your mind drift back a few years. During your elementary school days, what was the most popular sport played? At my school, I don't remember a day when we didn't play kick-ball. For sure it was our favorite pastime. Yet I believe that even this most innocent game ended up emotionally wounding many precious little spirits.

I have forgotten how the two captains were selected, but the actual team selection itself still rings crystal clear. All the children would line up sideways to be in full view of the captains. From that point, the captains would take turns selecting person by person to be on their respective teams. While I was usually selected near the beginning of the process, I still have quite vivid memories of the mounting tension I felt, worried that I might not be among the first drafts. I remember inwardly chanting, *Please pick me. Please, please somebody pick me.* I did not want to suffer the humiliation of continually being passed over. By the time the line dwindled down to the last five or six kids, it was all too obvious that neither captain really wanted those who were left. However, they had no choice other than to accept them. With only two persons remaining and pointing directly at one of them, I can still hear the selecting captain say to the other captain, "OK, I'll take that one, and you take the other one." Sheepishly looking down at the pavement, those two kids would just sort of shuffle their way on over to join the rest of their teammates.

Now you tell me, is it possible to endure that sort of humiliation day after day without it leaving any long-term impact? These kids were met with constant rejection from their peers. And whether intentional or not, they were sent a message that was all too clear: *You bring no value to the team. I really don't want you, but . . . you are being forced on me.* Although it was only an innocent game of kick-ball, for some it was the beginning of a cycle of rejection. For others whose worlds were already colored with abuse, school became just one more place where their lack of value was reaffirmed.

In years to come, my little five-year-old grandson, Kyler, will probably not remember many of the specifics concerning his life right now. Yet I can tell you that he is such a little ham for compliments. When we praise him for even the smallest acts, his face lights up with a shine that illuminates the entire room. When we praise him we are speaking directly to his need to feel valued. If we fail to notice his little drawings, or the brushing of his hair (only after he has first sprayed it really well with window cleaner), or whatever act he feels is deserving of praise, he will come to us, tug on our clothing, and insist that we stop what we are doing and notice his accomplishments. Of course, he knows that we are going to respond immediately with bunches of hugs, kisses, and high-fives as we proudly exclaim, "Good job, Kyler!"

Children like Kyler who receive positive affirmation at home are better able to handle not being among the first picks for a game of ball. I am not suggesting that it doesn't wound their little egos, but the consistent, warm, loving environment that is fostered at home will counterbalance and hopefully outweigh any outside negative experiences. How many times have I held and soothed my own children as they tearfully disclosed their little wounds? Assurance of my love and confidence in them somehow provided them with what they needed to believe in themselves in spite of the negative messages that they had received from those outside of our family circle.

As adults, we are no different. We are bound to encounter rejection in some form or another; and, when we do, we are going to need someone to be there who will soothe our wounds and affirm our self-value. We will need someone whose belief in us is so great that it literally has the power to help restore our belief in ourselves.

If your world is one of abuse and a cruel tearing down of self-esteem rather than a building up, and there is no one to speak positively into your life, I am a witness that God Himself will speak directly into your spirit if only you will allow Him. Perhaps your negative feelings toward yourself have been years in the making, and emotional abuse has been a very real part of your life for as far back as you can remember. Yet you must know that God sees and He cares. He so desperately wants to help you, but you must entrust yourself into His hands.

I shared with you concerning a season when my life was very torn and shattered. I really wasn't sure if I could turn things around or not. The mess that I had managed to make seemed insurmountable. But there were people whom God had strategically placed around me for such a time in which I found myself. They began ministering to me the healing love of God. As I listened to their message, the Holy Spirit began working in me, giving me the strength and the confidence to pick myself up and to try at life one more time. My very first step toward rebuilding was to commit my life wholeheartedly to the Lord. I pledged that I would live by His word. I wasn't sure what would come out of the whole Christian thing. It was all so new to me, and I really didn't have a good handle on precisely what to expect. But my life was so very broken. Having nowhere else to turn, I gave God a try. Now I can honestly say that He has blessed me above all that I ever dared dream or ask. Through the years I have learned that when we sincerely walk upright before God, He gets involved in all that concerns us, actively working at all times on our behalf.

So here is my question to you: Will you give God a try? I know you feel that your situation is hopeless, but will you try just one more time? I know you feel that no one cares and that nothing good ever works out for you, but please, please try. Just as God sent someone to me with a healing word, He has sent me to you. You must not quit on life. You must not succumb to a state of emotional numbness, refusing to feel. No matter what's going on around you and within you, you still can't give up. God will give you the strength and the conviction to believe in yourself—to believe in the destiny that He has placed within you. He will enable you to view yourself through His loving eyes. When there appears to be no one who will speak life into your spirit, God will speak! I know that He will because He spoke to me one day. And even right now as I write to you, He is yet speaking to all who will but listen.

Before going on to the next chapter, I want to share a little nugget that I believe will help you. I don't know how familiar you are with Old Testament biblical history; but, all throughout, God never allowed the enemy nations to completely wipe out His chosen people, Israel. Often battered, scarred, and even enslaved, yet never were they completely destroyed. God has always been faithful to leave a remnant, and that remnant has always been enough to build upon. Although you feel as if you have nothing left, you feel you have no value, you feel you have no worth—God always leaves a remnant. You are God's precious chosen. In spite of how it appears, in spite of how you feel at this current moment,

He did not allow the enemy to wipe you out completely. I promise you there is enough left within that you can build upon. Will you try?

Prayer:

Surrounded by such ugly pain and abuse, Father, never did I consider that You were there all the time. It was You who kept the enemy from completely destroying my life. Thank You for your faithfulness. For the first time in a long time, I can now sense a glimmer of hope, and I am willing to try at life again. I really want to be happy and to succeed. I desire relationships that will edify and build and not tear me down. Knowing that You have the perfect plan for my life, help me to yield my complete self over to You. Give me an ear to hear and a heart that longs to obey. Father, speak a healing word down in my soul and spirit. And this time around, I promise to wait on You. Amen.

Deeper Insights

1. *Self-value is not a sole matter of what we think of ourselves. It is largely our perception of what others think, feel, and say about us.*

I remember once being in a pretty heated conversation with a particular lady. All of a sudden, with venomous eyes, she looked at me and snarled, "You look at me like I'm trash!" To that statement I very calmly replied, "That's not at all what I think of you. That's what you think of yourself."

Emotional wounding and ongoing abuse damage our ability to properly perceive. As we are attempting to find a sense of value, it is only natural to look to others, at least in part, for some sort of gauge or measurement for that value. However, the danger is that as we look to them, we then are left to interpret (or misinterpret) the measurements, which are their thoughts and feelings concerning us. And because inner-wounds so distort perception, it makes an accurate reading of the measurements almost impossible.

Now I want you to re-read the statement in italics, keying in on the portion that deals with our perception of what others think, feel, and say about us. In light of that statement, ponder on the following questions:

How do you tend to view things in general? Is your world clouded with darkness? What is your general outlook? Is it more negative than positive?

If you find that your view is usually shaded by darkness, more than likely, your inner wounds are hindering your ability to see light. Through pain-tinted lenses, you perceive that others are looking down upon you. However, the truth is that there are many who hold you in high esteem and that greatly admire your strength and fortitude to move forward with life in spite of the many challenges.

2. *We must be extra cautious and carefully screen those persons that we allow to become a part of our inner circle. Once inside your inner circle, whether positively or negatively, building up or tearing down, they absolutely are going to speak into your life and your self-value will be impacted by their words.*

I teach the teens at my church every Tuesday evening. The setting is an open forum where everyone is free to discuss pretty much any and everything. Because I realize the enormous peer pressure to conform to worldly standards, I spend a great deal of time drilling foundational truths about opposite sex relationships. I emphatically advise my teens against casual dating. If his or her prospective mate is not someone who would make a good marriage candidate, then it is a mistake to enter into a dating relationship, no matter how harmless it may appear. Why? It is so easy to get lost in emotions, finding that they have taken over all sense of sound judgment and common logic. During our class sessions I often drill the teens, asking very direct questions: *The person you are considering dating, what are they accustomed to seeing in the home? Is it a single parent home where the mom works all day to provide for the children and then wearily hobbles home to attend to the cleaning, cooking, and mending?* I also inquire if their mates are in a situation where there is some form of ugly, ongoing abuse in the home. If so, I warn that abuse emotionally damages each and every offspring in the home. Furthermore, those who have lived in abusive environments, especially for extended time periods, are more likely to mimic that very same abusive behavior. I teach my teens that they absolutely must stop blindly pulling people into their intimate circle.

Love alone is not enough to build a solid, strong relationship. The mind is ever evolving, ever growing, ever expanding. It's just the way God made us. When we are young with no real responsibilities and no real direction, love is grand. But as we begin to mature and our minds begin to shift and turn towards the direction of our God-given destiny, will our mates be flowing in that same general direction also? Do the two of us share like passions, convictions, and goals? If not, our separate growth patterns will pull us apart, not together, and the days ahead will be filled with much turbulence.

Just know that most people will return to their roots. When you get pass your rebellious years and return to your wholesome Christian upbringing, to what kind of upbringing will your mate be returning? While you're walking through your home professing God's word, what choice words will your mate be releasing into the air waves?

Can two walk together, unless they are agreed? (Amos 3:3)

Chapter Two

And Her Desire Shall Be Unto . . . .

I want to get straight to the heart of the matter, and there is no better way than to share a particular conversation that took place around three years ago. I had just completed my broadcast, which at that time aired live. Right as I signed off the air, I received a phone call from a most distraught female caller. I could tell that she really needed someone to listen, so I sat attentively as she began to pour out all of her problems.

First order of business—her children were weighing very heavily on her mind. She lacked the resources to support them in the manner that she desired, which made her feel somewhat inadequate as a parent. Even small things, such as getting them to and from school, had become a real challenge. Also, the school was contacting her rather frequently concerning the children's behavior. Having little to no family or friend support, basically, she was on her own. I guess she had reached her limit the day that she phoned me. I once had been a single parent, so I could identify, as well as sympathize, with her. After about thirty minutes of venting the many frustrations that come along with being a single parent, she then moved on to her next issue.

It seemed that every man who had ever been a part of her life, in one way or another, had abused her. From relationship to relationship, from abuse to abuse—it seemed that she could not break that vicious cycle. Even the particular day that we spoke, she was in the midst of ending yet another abusive relationship. However, although she knew it was in her and the children's best interest to bring closure, she missed this particular man very much. As she continued talking, she even began to justify his abusive nature. I could tell that the relationship was probably far from being over. I could only listen and advise. The decision was hers to make.

By this time she was really sobbing. After about an hour of talking about problem after problem, she finally got to what I considered to be the real crux of the matter. For whatever reasons, her female neighbors did not seem to care for her. They took every available opportunity to make little snide, cutting remarks. Ignoring them as best she could, they finally broke her down with a comment that cut her to the very core of her being. Sneering down their noses at her in a way that only women can do, they said, *"Look at her. She ain't nothing. She ain't even got no man."*

Although violently abusive, this man, or any man for that matter, was the source for her value. If there was no male presence, she had no value. Apart from a man she was reduced to nothing through the eyes of her female neighbors and through her own eyes as well. Now, I can only imagine what you must be thinking. But before you pass judgment, let's talk about it.

When Adam and Eve disobeyed God in the Garden of Eden and ate of the forbidden fruit, what was the judgment sentenced against Eve? "*To the woman he said, 'I will greatly increase your pains in childbearing; with pain you will give birth to children. Your desire will be for your husband, and he will rule over you'*" (*Genesis 3:16 NIV*).

Pay close attention to the latter part of the verse: *"Your desire will be for your husband and he will rule over you."* For the female, there is a created place within her that only her husband can speak to. She literally longs and aches for him and for his touch. It goes far, far beyond a simple wanting. It is a deep-seated desire within that has the power to dominate and control her every thought.

The woman longs to be affirmed by her mate. Her desire—is unto him. She often craves and anxiously anticipates being in his presence. She loves leaning on his rugged dominance. Going to great lengths to please and make him happy, it causes her great pain to feel as though she has disappointed him or somehow failed him. For the most part, the female really does accept the male place of headship over her. In fact, not only does she accept it, she actually enjoys it. Being the head is such a natural position for him to assume; after all, God gave it to him. Submitting unto her mate's authority, she readily looks to him for her assignment of value. And generally speaking, she is willing to accept humbly whatever value he deems appropriate to assign.

The referenced scripture specifically addresses the married female's desire for her male counterpart. However, whether married or simply dating, there are certain principles and truths that remain constant. They are somewhat like spiritual governing laws that cannot be escaped. The curse that was placed on Eve has been passed down to all females, whether married or single. Women, without regard to their marital status, yearn for male validation. In the absence of such, their self-esteem and self-value often suffer. It is very natural for the female to feel incomplete or unfulfilled when there is no male presence in her life. There is just something about the male voice and the male touch that is able to reach way down and soothe the inner spirit of a woman. It really is the way that she was created. Even little girls, who are far from maturity, recognize and respond to both the authority and the comforts that masculinity brings.

Is this a good thing? Is it good that the man has this kind of dominant control (much of which is emotional) over his female partner? First we must consider the bible's intended audience. It was written to God's chosen people who were to live their lives within the very specific, detailed boundaries that He set forth. Within those boundaries, the man was instructed how to care for and provide for his wife. He was not to abuse her in any manner nor treat her harshly. He was told to cherish her like he cherishes his own body. Most powerful of all, the man was admonished to love his wife with the same intensity that

Christ loved the church and gave His life for it. Just think about that. One who loves you enough to give his very life for you, is it likely that he is going to demean your value by being harsh and cruel? Is it likely that he is going to abuse you physically, sexually, or emotionally? In my mind, true love is its own greatest controller. It will control the words that you speak and the tone in which you speak them. It will also cause you to evaluate and to control your actions.

One evening as my husband was teaching on marriage, he admonished the couples to act within the confines of their love for each other. He said if your love for your spouse allows you to talk to them and to treat them in any old manner, by all means, *do what your love will allow you to do.* I can assure you that everyone sitting there that night really, really heard the message. It was crystal clear. There was no room for error as it worked conviction in us all.

If you invest your emotions in a relationship that is not rooted in Christ and built around His word, you are setting yourself up to be hurt. If not the word of God, what will be the governing discipline in your union? Who will draw the boundary lines? Where there are no boundaries, everything is permissible; and, where everything is permissible, someone is bound to suffer great pain. Although excuses can be offered, the truth is that there are certain things that love in its purest form just does not do. There are certain tones and words that love just does not speak. Here is the bottom line in all of this: If someone says that they love you, that love should not cause you continual, non-ending emotional pain. Love should not hurt—not all the time anyway! Once again I reiterate: You must learn to screen carefully those you allow into your inner circle.

Dealing with Infidelity

Different does not mean better. In fact, different does not even mean equal to or as good as. Different just means different. Nothing more! Nothing less! Yes, a third party, an outsider has been brought into a relationship that was meant for only two. She is very different from you because she is not you. Yet, you must never lose sight of the fact that although different from you, she certainly is not better than you. Again, different does not mean better. It just means different.

I know how infidelity can bring about feelings of rejection, ugliness and loneliness: Rejection because for a given moment in time your partner has chosen another over you, even if only temporarily. Ugliness because you feel if only you looked better or if only you had the perfect figure, then certainly your partner would have never even been tempted to look at another. Loneliness because your spouse is out enjoying the company of another (or so you assume) while you are at home all alone miserably sobbing. You feel betrayed because your trust has been violated, and you feel like a failure because surely there should have been something that you could have done to keep your partner faithful to you.

There are endless factors that can bring stress into a marriage: financial hardships, different religious convictions, controlling and manipulative personalities, different views on how the children should be raised, different interests, likes, and passions. Although this is not by any means an exhaustive list, the factors sited are among the leading causes that can crumble the walls of a marriage, if allowed. In the mind of at least one spouse, hardships and challenges in a marriage are justifiable reasons for infidelity. Then there are others who have no particular reason for their unfaithfulness other than they just don't understand the sacred nature of the marriage covenant. Note here that I did not say one spouse chooses to ignore the sacredness; rather, one spouse does not understand the sacredness. Allow me to explain.

Marriage is a most holy and sacred institution. Two very separate and distinct persons, one male and one female, are presented before God. While standing there in His holy presence, the couple vows their abiding love and loyalty to each other—forsaking all others. They promise to cherish one another and to attend wholeheartedly to each other's needs. Before God, they pledge their total, complete selves to one another—their love, their faith, and their devotion. The vows, which are verbally spoken, are the official marriage covenant. The ceremony concludes with the couple retreating to their chosen place of privacy; and, there upon the marriage bed, the covenant is sealed by blood.

The blood of a sacrificed animal most often sealed biblical covenants. It was the force and the power behind that which had been agreed upon verbally. On the wedding night, as the married couple shared in their very first intimate encounter, the hymen (small membrane enclosing the female vagina) would rupture. Blood would then flow over the two of them thereby sealing and putting into force the marriage covenant. No longer were they two; they had been made one. The evening carried with it a far greater significance than that of mere physical pleasure. It was a time when their very spirits would be bonded and connected together as they gave themselves over so completely to one another. Just to think that God would make it possible for the husband and the wife to seal their marriage covenant with blood—it is all so very beautiful. He has such a perfect plan for marriage. Undeniably, it is His sacred institution.

Knowing each other's thoughts, sensing the other's pains, feeling your mate's presence even when they are nowhere around—these all testify to the spiritual nature of marriage. Then there are other occurrences, though not as pleasant, which also attest to the spiritual nature. Have you ever wondered why some remain in marriage unions that are obviously unhappy? Even in abusive relationships, it is often quite hard for one spouse just to pick up and walk out. To leave is almost as if they are walking out on a part of themselves. Truthfully, they are because of the very special bonding that takes place during marriage. Before I go any further, I must clarify what I am saying. **Never would I tell anyone to remain in an abusive relationship, especially one that is a threat to physical safety.** However, I am saying that I fully understand why leaving is not such a thing of ease. I believe that marriage ties are the most difficult ties to sever because the two people literally become interwoven. If you are in the midst of an unhappy or abusive relationship, I sincerely pray that God would grant you the wisdom to know what you must do and the courage to do it! *Listen for His voice. He will direct your steps.*

Those who have no spiritual relationship with the Lord, how can they understand the sacredness of marriage as I have just explained? They have no capacity to discern spiritual matters. The whole of their existence is spent in isolation apart from God. They have no communion with Him, and there is no real thought about living upright before Him.

I emphatically trust my husband. I believe that he is faithful to me. However, the confidence that I have in him has very little to do with me as a person or my abilities as a wife, but it has all to do with my husband's very personal desire to live upright before the Lord. An awesome love for God fills his heart. And although I occupy a very special place in his heart, his love for God also occupies that exact same space. In fact, it even overlaps and extends way beyond the boundaries of his love for me. Therefore, it is his love for God that keeps him faithful and that governs his actions towards me. I am not counting on my husband's love for me to keep him faithful. I am counting on his love for God! That is why the bible says that believers should not join themselves together with unbelievers (II Corinthians 6:14). When you go against this command and marry an unbeliever, at the point where your spouse's love for you ends, what is there to keep him from stepping outside the covenant?

Avoid Third Party Confrontations

The third party that your spouse has brought into the marriage, you happen to run across her address and phone number. What are you going to do with this newly found information?

You decide to call. You introduce yourself. Much to your surprise, you are met with total civility. The *other person* is most apologetic and assures you that she was totally unaware. She convinces you that she would never date someone who is married and promises that the relationship will be brought to an immediate, screeching halt.

GREAT! WONDERFUL! However, what did you really accomplish? Did you alleviate the problem?

Please remember, the third party did not walk into your marriage; she was brought in. Therefore, she is only a symptom. Your spouse is the problem. This time the confrontation with the *other person* went smoothly because she obviously had a conscience and a sense of moral integrity. However, what about the next time? (There will be a next time.) What about that one who will be brash and blatantly arrogant? She does not care that she is having an affair with your spouse, and neither does she care that you know. In fact, she is glad that you know. In a deranged sort of way, the whole ugly situation speaks to her need for value. After all, your spouse did leave you to come to her (even if just for an hour). What will your response be? Will you be able to maintain your composure, or will you allow yourself to be pulled into a nasty altercation?

Think it through before you confront that *other person*. What has been done, you cannot change. You can't change the past. However, you can shape the future course of events, where you are concerned anyway. Determine in your heart that you will maintain your dignity. Absolutely refuse to stoop and dirty yourself in someone else's mess. I know it's easier said than done because you are hurting, and you feel as if you must do something to relieve the pain. I know your very inner self feels as if it has been literally crushed and shattered into countless pieces. Yet, in the face of all the hurt and pain, carefully, carefully weigh and think through your actions. Do you really believe that there is any lasting benefit in treating symptoms? The problem is not going to cease until the root cause is properly dealt with, which in this case is your spouse. Only the two of you made vows to each other and committed yourselves to one another. Only the two of you sealed the marriage covenant. The *other person* never entered into a sacred union with you. She never pledged her loyalty to you. Your spouse did.

Indeed, it cannot be denied that infidelity does have a way of making people question their value. The humiliation and open shame that is thrust upon the innocent spouses makes them feel small and less than adequate in their own eyes. They wonder what others are saying. They feel they have to cover up and pretend that everything is O.K. Then there is always the matter of the bedroom. Do they still want to be . . . should they be . . . intimate with their spouse? Will they loathe the very touch? What if they become infected with some horrible disease?

Whether to continue in intimacy or not is a decision that only you will be able to make. I honestly believe if you seek God, He will lead you. That is His promise to all who belong to Him. Just know that whatever you decide, you have absolutely no reason to feel ashamed. It is your spouse; therefore, you are the one—the only one—with true intimate rights. *After much prayer, you will be empowered to make the right decision.*

Please be persuaded in your own heart and mind that your spouse's unfaithfulness has nothing to do with your value as a person. You must mentally rehearse this over and over again until it literally saturates your very spirit. Infidelity does not reflect, alter, nor address your value. It calls into question the integrity and morals of your spouse and the third party that has been brought into the marriage. It is themselves that they are degrading, and it is their character that they are damaging. Not yours. While you probably will feel the weight of the burden, just know that you are not devalued because of it. You must purposely decide to adjust your thinking, refusing to think less of yourself because of decisions that others are making. What another does, thinks, feels, or says does not change the person you are; it does not alter your created inner beauty, nor does it touch the value that God has invested in you. Who has the power to undo, to change, or to take away from what God has done?

You owe it to yourself and your marriage to assess and identify, as best you can, exactly where the break down between you and your spouse occurred. As you go through this process, be completely honest and acknowledge your shortcomings. Be willing to accept responsibility for your part in the problems that exist; however, be careful not to accept or internalize blame that does not rightfully belong with you.

Also, make sure that you don't torture and brow beat yourself by continually wallowing in thoughts of *if only you could have been more, done more, said more, had more . . . .* Don't do that to yourself. It is a self-destructive exercise, yielding no profit. If we are honest, there are situations in every marriage that could have been handled in a more appropriate manner. We all have made decisions which, over a period of time, proved not to be the most beneficial. In such instances, my consolation is that at the time when the decision was made, I honestly believed that I was acting in the best interest of all involved. The point is that, at some time or another, we all have missed the mark and made mistakes. Learning from those mistakes, we earnestly commit to do better, and we move forward.

While human frailties and mistakes made may provide convenient excuses, they are not justification for infidelity. The institution of marriage is holy and must be treated as such. The marriage covenant goes beyond the loyalty that we owe to our spouses. More importantly, it embraces an understood loyalty to God. Marriage is His institution, and it is not entered into separate and apart from His presence.

Prayer:

Father, through Your Spirit at work in me, I can be the spouse that You have called me to be. While I cannot control my mate's actions, I believe that as I live out Your presence in me, You will empower me to become a force of influence. Father, bless my everyday living to be a shining message of Your love and kindness to those in my home. Radiate through me and bring to naught every evil plan that has been set against my marriage. Amen.

Deeper Insights

Most powerful of all, the man was admonished to love his wife with the same intensity that Christ loved the church and gave His life for it.

My husband does such an awesome job teaching the men in our church concerning their God-given roles in the home. In almost thirty years of sitting under various ministries, I have never heard any teaching that surpasses his as it relates to that particular subject matter. After hearing his message, single women walk away fully armed, knowing what they should look for in a Godly mate. And men, both married and single, walk away challenged to perform and live up to the standards that God has ordained in His word. They are called to rise up and be men, true leaders in the home, worthy of respect. Allow me to share with you a few of the highlights from my husband's teachings.

Although it is seldom considered, the institution of marriage is meant to be a symbol or a replica of the relationship that Christ has with the church. In scripture, Christ is often referred to as the groom; and the church, which is comprised of every born again believer, is His bride. The following verses of scripture are a glorious portrait of marriage. They are the foundation and the support of my husband's beliefs and teachings. Please carefully read them through:

> *Husbands, love your wives, just as Christ loved the church and gave himself up for her to make her holy, cleansing her by the washing with water through the word, and to present her to himself as a radiant church, without stain or wrinkle or any other blemish, but holy and blameless. In this same way, husbands ought to love their wives as their own bodies. He who loves his wife loves himself. After all, no one ever hated his own body, but he feeds and cares for it, just as Christ does the church—for we are members of his body. "For this reason a man will leave his father and mother and be united to his wife, and the two will become one flesh." (Ephesians 5:25-31 NIV)*

My husband says that as a single man, it was this particular passage of scripture that caused him the greatest concern as he pondered marriage. It was evident to him that God required that his love for his wife be totally selfless, and that he be willing to lay down his very life in exchange for her safety and protection. He teaches that until a man can settle this particular issue and come to an internal peace, accepting the weighty responsibility, then he is not ready to be joined in the bonds of holy matrimony. Having made this point crystal clear, he then moves forward to teach on the husband's role in the home.

The husband is charged by God to be the provider and the overall caregiver. He is not to be a lord or dictator forcing his family into submission. Rather, he is to preside lovingly over his household. As the one who presides, his job is to assess, encourage, and inspire the natural gifts and talents of all that are within his house. In addition, it is also his job to ensure that those gifts and talents are brought to a point of maximum development. As entrusted steward over his home, he is to make certain that all who are under his charge—his wife and children—achieve their full God-given potential. Whatever personal sacrifices he must make to ensure that his family is brought to a point of brilliance, then that is his God-given charge as leader over the home. And his own personal success should be visible only through the veil of his family's successes.

Now let's take a few moments and note what Christ, the bridegroom, did for His bride. He died for her. He willingly surrendered His life, which is the ultimate sacrifice, so that He might perfect His bride. He endured grief, agony, and shame that He might confer upon her a state of being—*holiness*—which she was not able to attain on her own. He lovingly and patiently washed her with His word to make her clean. This, He did that His bride might be presented to Him in brilliance, having neither blemishes nor spots nor any such imperfections. His all sacrificed at Calvary, He brought her into a glorious place, which she did not have the capacity to reach apart from Him. Because of His sacrificial love, she became blameless and perfected before the Heavenly Father. With this picture of marriage clearly in view, what space is there for abuse within its sacred bonds?

Chapter Three

Changing Your View

How well do I remember the evening that my husband, Daniel, asked me to marry him. When we met I was living in government project housing with my two very young children, Stacy and McKenzie. A victim of a failed marriage, my less than desirable living conditions had caused me to grow somewhat pessimistic concerning my future. As much as I dreaded the possibility, I really wasn't sure that anything good or positive was going to work out for me. I couldn't imagine how things could possibly turn around. All of my days seemed to be lined with a dismal gloom. It was my faithful companion, and I had grown rather accustomed to its dreary presence. I hoped for something better . . . I wanted something better. But just as I would dare to dream, the voice of reality within would ask, *what could there possibly be for me?* Never, not once, did it fail to remind me of my past, and it also made sure that I never forgot that it was my own bad decisions that had landed me in my current predicament. Yet in all of its speaking, day in and day out, never, not once, did it bother to encourage me that there was a new day dawning for the children and me, and it was just beyond the horizon.

I was definitely a woman with a lot of history, none of which would have qualified me as the ideal marriage candidate to a United States Army officer. Nonetheless, God saw something that obviously went far beyond what I saw (and I am sure what many others saw as well). The evening that my husband proposed was so very special. He expressed his love for me as well as his sincere desire to provide and to care for me. Gazing into my eyes, he then asked if he could have my hand in marriage. What followed next is indelibly written in my heart as my all-time most cherished memory. Yet looking directly into my eyes, he continued his proposal: "I am not just asking you to be my wife; I want your children to be my children, and I want your bills to be my bills." You must know that there was nothing that could have ever prepared me for that moment. Never in my wildest dreams did I ever dare imagine that God had something so completely, totally wonderful for me! Someone else who had been more deserving, I could understand why He would bless them in such a manner—BUT ME? There were many days when I would just weep because I was so overcome by the magnitude of God's blessings in my life.

Although I was in the midst of what seemed to be a fairy tale, this new life presented me with a whole new set of challenges. Now the wife of an army officer, I felt that I had to measure up in a world where I couldn't. It was all so unfamiliar. Quite frequently we were called upon to attend various social events. These mandatory gatherings were just part of the territory that came along with being in the officer ranks. I really wanted to leave a good impression. I wanted to fit in among the other officer's wives, but I often felt awkward and out of place. I could only imagine what they would think of me if they knew the real truth of who I was. My past had left me with so much baggage, none of which did I care to disclose. For more years than I care to recall, I allowed my need to be valued, by these complete strangers, to control me, and at times even alter my behavior. Well, here I am now some twenty-four years later, and my need to be valued is still as strong as it has ever been. However, what has changed for me is that I no longer need that affirmation to come from those outside of my intimate circle. My husband truly was God's gift to me. From the beginning of our marriage up until this present day, he has consistently spoken into my life, into my destiny. When I saw no real value in myself, he did. Through his very gentle way with me, he has greatly contributed to my becoming the woman that I am. Yet, there is still a much bigger picture that I want to share with you.

In twenty-four years of marriage, my husband has never faltered in his conviction to live a Godly life and to model Godly behavior in our home. As I submitted to his headship and followed him, I was led into my own very intimate place with God. As I grew more and more comfortable in God's presence, He also began speaking into my life. (I am sure that He had been speaking all along. I just didn't know His voice.) Pleasing God became really important to me. The thought of letting Him down was more than I could bear. Even to this day, I still weep when I feel that I have not been the representative for Him that I should. It is important to me that as people observe my life, they get a clear, undistorted picture of who Christ is. At some point—I am really not sure exactly when it happened—the overwhelming need for people affirmation began to dwindle. I sought for God's affirmation. I wanted Him to be pleased with me, with my everyday living. He gave true meaning and purpose to my life. As I walked in closeness with Him, I became more in tune to my true inner being, the person I had been created to be. For the first time in my life, I could really see my inner value and worth. God assigned my value, and it was not based on anything external (possessions, status, education). It flowed directly out of my relationship with Him as He lived and operated through me. His living inside of me was the very source and core of my total worth.

As a new officer's wife, I felt I had to do something, have something, or be something in order to be a woman of value. Please don't fall into that trap. There isn't a feat that you will ever accomplish or a height of status that you will ever reach which can give you true inner value. You will only find it as you allow Christ's presence to live in and flow through you. Your value will not come through anything external; it will come through the internal dwelling of Christ, living and making His home inside of you. Stop looking for value outside of yourself. Look within.

Changing Your View

People often wait in long lines, pay exorbitant sums of money, and arrive many hours in advance to ensure select seating at some favored event. Why are they willing to go to such lengths? Pure and simple, many want what is commonly referred to as *a bird's eye view*. A bird's view is most often aerial, allowing for a much broader range of scope. Imagine standing on the ground looking out as far as you can see. Now imagine yourself looking out of a window which is on the 10th floor. From the 10th floor, your view will be much wider, fuller, and comprehensive. Standing right beside an object, at best, you will only be able to see very small segments—pieces of a whole. However, an aerial view allows you to see a considerably greater portion, possibly the whole.

This whole concept of a bird's eye view was really driven home for me when my husband, my son, and I went to the movies. I had long awaited the release of a particular Christian film, and I wanted to make sure that I was there on opening night. Arriving at the movies, we found that there were many others who also had been awaiting its coming. It was a packed theater. The only remaining seats were few and far in between, well except for those on the front row. For whatever the reason (which soon I was to find out), in the front there were quite a few vacant seats. My husband secured the needed seats for our family; and, after getting popcorn and drinks, my son and I came in joined him.

After only a few minutes into the movie, I knew there was no way I could stay in that front row seat and enjoy the movie. It was a horrible view. In order to see anything at all I had to look up and position my head back in an awkward sort of manner, which in turn placed a most uncomfortable strain on my neck. There was no way I could endure that discomfort for two hours. And as if the strained neck was not enough, because I was sitting so close, I found that I couldn't even see the entire screen, only a very small section. I had waited too long for the release of that film. Anxiously, I had anticipated opening night all week. Determined that I was not going to miss out, I told my husband that I was going to move to another seat. Sitting on that lowest level hindered my view, and there was only one way for me to experience the fullness of the film. I was going to have to change my position and move up higher. Leaving my husband and son sitting on the front row,

I climbed up several more levels before finally settling down. From my new higher location, I had a bird's eye view.

If ever you are to see yourself for the true jewel that God has created you to be, you must make a deliberate decision to change the way you think and the location from where you are currently viewing. You cannot stay at ground level and have God's eye view. To see as God sees requires that you climb and look from the place where He is looking. It is only in His presence where you will be empowered to see as He sees.

What kind of view did Abraham have as he drew back his hand to slay his son, Isaac, in an act of holy worship (Genesis 22:3-14)? Knowing that his son was the sacrifice that God required, where was he really standing when he told his servants that he and Isaac were going to worship but they would return? Did he see that on the Mount of the Lord, God Himself would provide His own sacrifice? What kind of view enabled a loving mom to respond that all was well when her only son had just died in her arms (II Kings 4:15-36)? From where was she looking as she took the dead boy and laid him on the bed of the prophet, Elisha? What did she see? Is it possible that she was standing in a place where even death itself had to bow in subjection to a higher power—the highest power? What was her view? While being stoned, exactly what was Stephen's view as he saw the heavens roll back revealing Jesus as He stood on the right hand side of His Father (Acts 7:54-60)? Where was he standing?

When looking at your situation, if all you see is gloom and hopelessness, then you must be willing to change your view. Climbing higher to another level will enable you to gain a much wider scope of vision. Although there may not be an immediate change in your situation, there will be an immediate change in your perspective. As you climb into God's presence, you will be enabled to see a broader, fuller picture. You will see that all of the isolated pieces of your life (or so you thought they were isolated) have been skillfully woven together. You will be allowed to see that there is a set time for your pain to cease and that a far greater good than you could have ever imagined is being worked through it. I honestly don't believe that it is truly possible to enter into God's presence and not receive His awesome gift of hope. As you get a glimpse of what He sees, your hope will be restored, and it will be renewed. Sitting right within reach, this precious gift of hope will be yours for the taking. *Don't be afraid to reach out and lay hold. He wants you to have it. You safely can trust in the hope that God offers. All that He reveals, it will surely come to pass.*

As you climb your way up, you will see that what you are experiencing right now is only a small portion of the entire view; it is not the whole picture. Quite contrary to what the enemy wants you to believe, God has not forgotten you, and He does have a plan for your life. I know that your pain might have begun when you were a small child and has seemingly been non-ceasing as you went from one bad experience to another. However, I am yet saying that if you would just dare to climb, there is another view. God's view is always different from our view, and we cannot see as He sees unless we join Him where He is. Where you are currently standing, you will never be able to see past your pain. Everywhere you turn, it will be there to obstruct your vision. Stop looking around; look up.

> *I lift up my eyes to the hills—where does my help come from? My help comes from the LORD, the Maker of heaven and earth. (Psalm 121:1-2 NIV)*

Too weak to climb

Alone in the projects with two small children, I could not see that anything positive or life changing was going to happen for me. I grew up in a middle class neighborhood where, generally, both parents were present in the home. Thinking back, there were very few single-parent homes in our community. I was an only child, and my parents were able to provide very well for me. After I grew up and had children of my own, it was only natural that I would want to provide them with a similar lifestyle, if not better. However, the welfare check that I was receiving did not lend itself to a life of luxury. It covered only the bare essentials.

I remember many days of feeling that my life was over. Around and around in a circle, just going through meaningless, mundane, never-ending motions—that was the location where my bad decisions had taken me. Then totally against my will, I had been dumped off and abandoned. Yet the saddest, most unfortunate part of it all was not so much the fate that I had been left to suffer, but I had two precious little people, my girls, who were looking to me with such trust in their eyes. What had I done to my babies? They deserved so much more than I was able to give, financially and, even more importantly, emotionally. I wished that I had made different choices. Truly a kid playing grown-up, how was I to know that with each choice I made, I actually was building a house (more like a prison) for the children and for me? And how was I to know that once the house was completed, we would be forced to move in? Oh, how I wanted to leave that place. I wanted to see a different picture. I wanted a clearer view, but I had no strength. I felt too weak to climb.

Sometimes your dwindling strength won't allow you to jump right into the ring full force. The good news is—YOU DON'T HAVE TO! If you can just manage to collect and squarely focus your thoughts on God, then that is, in fact, the first step toward changing your view. And as you become aware that your thoughts are shifting back to your current dilemma, you must seize them immediately and place them back on God. Sometimes lying in my bed weeping, over and over again, I would repeat: *"You will keep him in perfect peace, Whose mind is stayed on You, Because he trusts in You"* (Isaiah 26:3). I literally had to force the negative thoughts away and replace them with God's word. It was such a spiritual battle, and it was very real work on my part to fight. Through the salty, flowing tears, at night I would often repeat that verse until I finally fell asleep. God saw me earnestly trying, and He met me at the point of my need. I am a witness that His strength really is made perfect in our weaknesses. Although I was in pain, I did feel His calming presence. I knew that I wasn't alone.

When we do all we can and have no more strength left, He is faithful to step in and complete what we lack. When you feel as if you can't climb, just think on Him. Earnestly fight to bring your thoughts under subjection, refocusing them on God's word. Read your bible, increasing your study and meditation time bit by bit everyday. Choose some key passages that specifically speak to your situation. Stand firm on His word, verbally repeating key passages throughout the day. His word is alive. As we fully ingest it into our systems, it will cleanse and purify; it will restore and make whole.

Although the pain of your situation may press you down, you must make a conscience decision that it is not going to take you under. The Lord will be faithful to send others into your life to inspire and encourage you as you climb to another level. Yet, ultimately, the climb is still yours to make. Your emotional health is your responsibility. Be careful not to place undue stress on friendships by trying to shift that burden. As you take the lead in the fight, those who love and are concerned about you will want to join in and assist. However, continually remind yourself of their role in your life. They are there only to help, not to take the lead. It is your fight and the lead belongs to you.

On your knees in communion with God, you must decide that you will climb to a location where death has no dominion. Where you are currently standing, death has laid claim to your self-esteem and to your sense of self-value and worth. It has also taken away your hope for a better tomorrow. It has seized your joy, your peace, and your desire for life. You must reach deep within yourself. There is a remnant of strength left, and you must use it climb. Climb to that place where death is commanded to loose its prey. Climb to that place where that loving mom stood. Her son died in her arms, yet she did not see death as being final. She knew of a place where death had no power nor did it have any authority. Be encouraged because there is such a place. It is high in the heavens, far from the reach of all that can bring you harm. It is your retreat from the storm. It is your shelter from the abuse that currently surrounds you. You will be safe there.

Prayer:

Father, empower me to soar to new heights, revealing a whole new world of possibilities. Allow me to be fed and nurtured by your indwelling presence. I want to see as You see. Gird me up and take me to that place. Amen.

Deeper Insights

1. *Truly a kid playing grown-up, how was I to know that with each choice I made, I actually was building a house (more like a prison) for the children and for me? And how was I to know that once the house was completed, we would be forced to move in?*

Every single week I remind the teens at my church that they are building a house. I tell them that every single decision they make—whether it's a decision to be sexually active, cut school, not do homework, be disrespectful to their parents, or teachers—they are in fact building a house. And once completed, they will be forced to move in. For every action there is an ensuing consequence. No one is allowed to live a reckless, careless life and get by. Neither can we live in direct opposition to God's word without penalties. Experience has taught me that strict adherence to God's word works an overall wellness of being, physically as well as emotionally. However, when we insist on living a lifestyle that is in direct violation to His statutes and commands, we will reap much hurt, pain, and suffering.

2. *The Lord will be faithful to send others into your life to inspire and encourage you as you climb to another level. Yet, ultimately, the climb is still yours to make. Your emotional health is your responsibility.*

Over the years I have noted a very common trait among those who have suffered great emotional damage. Whether intentional or not, there is a very definite tendency towards shifting the responsibility for their emotional health onto others. In the more extreme cases, the wounded party will often communicate messages such as, *I feel unhappy today. It is your responsibility to cheer me up. Whatever you have planned couldn't possibly be more important than spending time with me. After all, you know that I need someone to be there for me. You know all that I have been through.*

This kind of dependency is just too consuming for anyone to effectively manage—friend, family member, church associate, or whoever. It is just simply not fair to place such a heavy burden on another's shoulders, especially upon those whom we genuinely love and who genuinely love us in return. If we insist on doing so, it will only be a matter of time before the incredible drain and stress that it places on the relationship will become unbearable, forcing our loved ones to withdraw from us either emotionally, physically, or perhaps both. Solid, good relationships are very rare and should be highly treasured and protected. Both parties have mutual responsibility to share in those efforts. While a friend is born to aid in times of adversity (Proverbs 17:17), every single day should not be an adverse day. Lovingly releasing our loved ones, we must transfer the burden for our emotional health onto the only one strong enough to shoulder the heaviest of burdens day after day and still never grow weary. That one is Jesus Christ our Lord.

Chapter Four

Through God's Eyes

Incest . . .
Prostitution . . .
Lust . . .
Adultery . . .
Murder . . .

Who would have ever dared to imagine that such—*shall we say colorful*—traits would be woven into the lineage of our Lord and Savior, Jesus? Brilliant by design, these woven threads speak of God's ability and His desire to take our past failures, hurts, and mistakes and weave them into a work of compelling beauty. Only He can do it! Perhaps when you look at yourself you see no worth. However, when God looks at you, He sees a masterpiece. He knows every offense that you have ever committed, as well as those that have been committed against you. In spite of your past, when God looks at you He sees beauty, and He sees value. You are a treasured pearl of great price; after all, you are His handiwork. Unfortunately, the enemy also knows of your great value, which is the reason for his relentless attacks against your self-esteem. He refuses to let up, even for a moment, fearing that you might discover who you really are and what you are capable of accomplishing.

Although it will not be an easy task, we absolutely must change the way that we view ourselves—our self-perception. By whatever means necessary, we must begin to see ourselves as God sees us; and, just as important, we also must be willing to accept His view of us as absolute truth. It seems that everyone would be really eager to embrace a view where they are free from pain, happy, and fulfilled. Quite the contrary, it is utterly amazing how many people literally reject and push away anything or anyone that offers them hope. I make it a practice to sow into the lives of people, especially where their value and self-esteem are concerned. An expression of pride in their work, a pat on the back, a sincere hug—whatever I can do to make others feel good about who they are, I am all for it! More times than I care to recount, I have sown compliments only to have them immediately rejected and then sort of callously shoved back in my direction. When this happens, I know that it is not a premeditated response; rather, it is just an instinctive, natural reaction.

I remember one young lady in particular who, for the life of her, just could not receive a compliment. She honestly did not believe that she possessed any positive qualities. She felt that her little sister did, but not her. If I complimented her on a hairstyle or on a particular outfit that she happened to be wearing, not even allowing time for my words to register fully, she would immediately come back with a strong retort, saying, "No you don't! You don't like it! It's ugly!" It was as if her inner-self was barren. There was no life. Something deep within her obviously had been severely wounded; and, because of the immense damage suffered, her spirit now refused to grab hold to anything that could produce life. We must understand that barren does not address one's ability to give birth. Rather, it speaks to one's inability to conceive life. (This revelation of barrenness, as God imparted it to me, is fully discussed in Chapter 6.) Pain and emotional wounding have a way of creating this barren condition within its victims.

To see yourself as God sees you will require that you fully accept and believe all that He will reveal concerning you. His view of you is absolute truth. And only as you allow that truth to saturate your spirit, will it bring liberation, freeing you from the negative self-images of your past. Your thoughts concerning yourself may not change instantaneously. This is especially true if those negative thoughts have been years in the making. Yet, with a ferocious tenacity that refuses to be sidetracked, you must actively seek for God, continually asking Him to reveal His vision for your life. Seek Him until you are finally enabled to conceive, grabbing hold to and refusing to let go of the seed that He will plant deep within your being. If you can only receive the seed—the seed that will reveal who you really are and what you were meant to accomplish—life will spring forth.

You probably already have a pretty good idea of what others think and feel concerning you. However, what you probably don't so readily know is what God thinks. The cycle of negativity that others brought into your life eventually will be broken as you begin entertaining such questions as: *When God looks at me, exactly what does He see? What does He really think of me? How can I move to the place where He desires for me to be?* As you redirect your energies and earnestly search for these truths, you will be empowered to tear down all those old, negative self-images, replacing them with images that reflect the truth of exactly who God created you to be. As you accept and embrace yourself as He sees you, your great value and worth will begin to shine through radiantly. No longer will His view be a hidden mystery to you. When God looks at you, what does He see? Allow me to start you on your journey as you begin your search for truth.

WHEN GOD LOOKS AT YOU HE SEES . . . PURPOSE

Being in full-time ministry, I meet many people. Among them there seems to be one common concern—they want to know their true purpose. They want to know specifically what they were put on earth to accomplish. Unsure of how to unfold this mystery, which they believe holds the absolute answer to all of their problems, I have witnessed many as they aimlessly spin out of control. They try their hand in one area and then quickly resort to another. Soon abandoning their latest undertaking, before long, they are off to yet another. So much movement, so much instability—it is all in the name of "finding purpose." Truthfully, I fear that ordained purpose in the minds of many has become synonymous with acquisitions, the ability to buy things.

Seems a bit ironic, but in a day where there is such an abundance of material goods, the emotional state of the masses seems to be that of unhappiness, loneliness, discontentment, and depression. I don't ever recall depression being as widespread as it now appears to be. At some point it seems that we would come to accept the reality that "things" cannot bring happiness. It is only as we walk daily in God's purpose for our lives that we will experience true inner-peace and contentment.

While we are spinning on our heels anxiously looking in every direction for purpose, it is most often right before us. Every single day of our existence is divinely packed and filled to capacity with purpose. Yet, most often, this daily purpose is overlooked. In search of grandeur, simplistic beauty escapes unnoticed; in anticipation of tomorrow, today is not fully experienced nor appreciated. Every morning when we awaken, divine purpose is there to greet us. But because it is neither what we anticipate nor particularly desire, it generally goes unnoticed and unfulfilled. It is only as we are faithful to fulfill our God given daily assignments that we graduate into the fullness of His call upon our lives. I want to share three of these very basic areas of purpose that most often are overlooked and unfulfilled.

Purpose in Rest

In the creation account as found in the first two chapters of Genesis, God created the heavens, the earth, and all that was within. For six days He created, and every single day held a specific focus which was different from the day before. Satisfied with all the works of His hands, on the seventh day we see yet another shift in focus. On the seventh day—*God rested.* He hallowed the day (consecrated and set it apart), forever establishing a period that men were to cease from their labor. As this day was observed, minds, bodies, and spirits were given opportunity to be refreshed and renewed. God's ultimate, divinely ordained purpose to be fulfilled on the seventh day was simply—rest.

There are times when I am so fatigued that I cannot offer God my best. Although I desire to do so, my body and my mind simply refuse to jump on board with my desires. I am positively committed to serving God in a spirit of excellence; but, when physical and mental exhaustion set in, I lose my ability to focus and stay on task. We have been conditioned to think that we must always be busy working, running here, running there, and running everywhere. Although we don't admit it, our self-value somehow erroneously has become tied into our much doing. Always doing, always giving, always supporting. However, we fail to realize that just because we are physically engaged does not mean that God is pleased with us, nor does it mean that we are accomplishing the specific assignment that He has entrusted to us for that particular season. Could it be possible that our true God-given purpose for a given time might be to set aside our busy schedules and calendars and simply rest? I sincerely believe that "rest" is often our destined purpose, and many times that purpose is grossly unfulfilled. A foreign thought for many, it really is possible that as you curl up comfortably with a great book or take a long afternoon nap, God is so very pleased. Finally, you are walking in your divinely ordained purpose—for that season anyway. The season of rest may be an hour, a day, or it may even be a week.

After a day or two of complete rest, my thoughts flow with greater ease, and my spirit is open and clear to receive from the Lord. I can hear His voice; I can feel His presence. After one such retreat, I returned home so refreshed. The overwhelming anxiety and stress that I was experiencing lifted; my mind was cleared, and I was enabled to begin the writing of this book. I knew that indeed the book was a God-ordained assignment. It filled my thoughts. Yet, my emotional state hindered me from getting started. Completely stressed, I checked into a local hotel on a Friday evening. I slept soundly through the night; and, with the exception of 3 to 4 hours, I slept all of Saturday away as well. I checked out Sunday morning fully prepared for worship service, both physically and emotionally. Not many days after, I sat down intent in purpose and began this book. When God looked at me that particular weekend, He saw ordained purpose. And clearly, the purpose that He saw was—REST! It was only after I fulfilled that call that I was empowered to move into my next assignment.

We all experience stress, some more frequently than others. Then there are those whose everyday lives are filled with a stressful tension that mounts and builds all throughout the day, not ending until it climaxes with some form of ugly abuse. If this happens to be your situation, God does have a shelter for you. He has a place where you can retreat and just rest—rest your mind, your body, and your spirit. He has ordained it for the refreshing of your entire self. He knows how desperately you need rest, and He will be faithful to provide. I pray with you and for you that as He reveals your secret place of get away, you will take the opportunity to enter in. That place may be in a soothing tub of very warm water filled with soft scents, or it may be in your car as you travel to and from work. Perhaps, it even may be in the office break-room area where you spend your lunch hour. I have learned that wherever we are, even if on a crowded bus, we can transform our little space into a private sanctuary just for two. There will be no one there but you and God, and you will be able to rest quietly in His presence. I know from personal experience that it is indeed possible, and I also know that you will leave refreshed. Although surrounded by masses, in quiet, peaceful solitude, I have often rested.

In vain you rise early and stay up late, toiling for food to eat—for he grants sleep to those he loves. (Psalm 127:2 NIV)

Purpose in Pain

We visited my mother-in-law, Mattie Gant, several times during her illness. Cancer had permeated her major organs. Her increasing level of pain and discomfort became more and more evident with each visit. After about five or six months of a very intensive battle, she passed. Throughout her illness, she stood solid in her faith. Although pain was consuming her body, I never witnessed her waiver nor falter in her convictions. She believed what she believed, and nothing, not even the bitter cruel ravages of cancer, was going to change that. She lived a Godly life that was above reproach, and all who knew her and had opportunity to observe her life clearly saw Christ as He operated through her daily walk. No one could argue that. Yet, everything that she had professed through the years had now come to its ultimate point of testing. She awakened to pain, fell asleep with pain, and often was prohibited from sleeping at all because of pain. How much can any one person be asked to endure?

During those months as she struggled for her life—body thin and frail as she lie confined to her bed—her ministry soared to new heights. There was divine purpose in her pain, and God used it to minister volumes to me and to many others as well. Let me share with you portions of her ministry during those last months of her life.

By the time the cancer was discovered, it already had spread throughout much of her body. The doctors were assessing what could be done. If they were unable to prolong life, at a minimum, they wanted to improve the quality of what remained, as much as they could anyway. Only a few days after we initially received the news of her condition, we left our home in Georgia and drove to Florida. Our first stop was the hospital where my mother-in-law had been admitted as a patient. My husband comes from a very large family, and most of his siblings and their children were already at the hospital when we arrived. As many of us crowded into her little room, I still remember the beautiful, gentle smile that adorned her face as she said, "Either way it goes, it's alright with me." I knew exactly what she meant. She was in total peace. She was ready to live. She was ready to die.

During the whole ordeal, never, not once, did I ever hear my mother-in-law complain. If anyone had a right to, certainly she did. I could not even begin to imagine pain on the level that she endured. Sometimes we so easily complain over such small, insignificant matters, yet here was a woman whose voice had been reduced to nothing more than a very faint whisper that you had to strain to hear. Throughout her struggle, I never heard her complain nor question her fate. She entrusted herself to God and she rested.

Obviously in excruciating pain, I saw as she so unselfishly endured the pain of touch and allowed her grandchildren to crowd around her bed for what was to be their final photo with their grand-mom. As they hugged and kissed on her, she whispered, "I love you" to them all. I was standing at the foot of her bed, soaking it all in, committing as much as I could to memory. I knew the cost of that precious gift. She experienced much pain as the children swung their arms around her. She thought it well worth the cost. It was her final gift to her beloved grandchildren.

Up until her very last breath, God had purpose for her life. He purposed that through her pain, many would see new dimensions of what it really means to trust in Him. We witnessed a love so strong as she willingly suffered, just that she might give a gift. Even from the grave, the life that she lived still speaks. Cancer ravaging her body, pain inflicting her very spirit—God looked at her and He saw purpose.

I hurt that you are hurting. I want all the hurt to go away and never return. I hate all that you have had to endure throughout your life. I feel a deep burden because of your pain. I know that in God's own time, He will deliver you. I won't pretend to understand why you've been subjected to certain abuses. However, even right now in the midst of your deep pain and trauma, God looks at you and He sees purpose. Right now where you are, He desires to use you. Don't allow the enemy to take you through all that you are enduring and God receive nothing from it. Satan means to destroy you; however, the very weapon that he has formed against you, God will use it to build you up. I know that this might be new thinking, perhaps even a bit radical, and I certainly know that I am not asking something that will be easily done. Seek God. Ask Him to be glorified in your life even as you ride out the storms. Ask Him to show you every opportunity where you may minister out of your pain. *Although you are hurting, depressed, sad, and feel like giving up, when God looks at you He sees value; He sees purpose.*

Purpose in Family

As a little girl growing up, I spent a tremendous amount of time at my grand-mom's. She lived in the country in a big white two-story house. As soon as you topped the big hill off the main paved road, you could see it. Its country charm and warmth reached out and met each visitor as they made their way down the graveled, dusty road. Even before entering the house, the atmosphere of home permeated the air.

My grand-mom was an awesome cook, and everybody, even from miles around, knew it. It was not unusual for her to fix huge meals on Sundays—the kind that you would expect on special holidays. I can't tell you how many times she or my Aunt Mat (who was also an awesome cook) would stand up in church and invite the entire congregation over for Sunday dinner. Between the two of them, these gatherings happened at least five to six times a year. Truthfully, I am sure that I am understating the frequency. They would both set formal tables: white linen tablecloths and napkins, fine china, sterling silver eating and serving utensils, elegant crystal water goblets, and tea glasses. As many as could be seated at the table would take their places, and then everyone else would disperse throughout the remainder of the house. More often than not, I remember having a place at the formally set table. Never, not once, do I ever recall my grand-mom asking me to move. My cousins and I were important to her, and she made sure that we knew it. We were not an inconvenience to her nor were we in the way. She made us feel as if we too were special guests. With love and patience, my grand-mom taught me how to prepare, as well as to eat from, a formal table.

While many, especially those in their early twenties and thirties, are frantically searching for purpose, I fear that they are looking right over top of it, literally. They fail to realize that those precious little ones who are twirling, dancing, skipping around their legs, and vying for their attention are the purpose—for that season anyway. Our children should not be made to feel that they are an inconvenience, nor should they be made to feel that they are in the way. For the most part, our plans should be scheduled around them, not them around our plans. They are the priority, and their best interest must heavily weigh in all decisions that we make, especially those decisions where they will be impacted directly.

Although we may be experiencing great success in our careers, as well as in the many other areas that bid for our time, if those activities are not our ordained purpose for that particular season, we will yet feel empty and incomplete. It is only as we submit to God's ordained purpose for our lives and walk in that purpose, that we will experience true inner contentment and fulfillment. Accepting that our children are in fact our divinely ordained purpose, the self-value and fulfillment that we seek will naturally flow forth as we successfully walk in that purpose, which in this case is to be a good parent.

It is impossible to separate our image from the image of our children. They are the accessories that adorn and complete our total presence. Although we may be perfectly and elegantly suited, if they look tattered and their clothing is tight, too short, and very dated, it is our image that will greatly suffer. When I see a mom or dad very neatly dressed, with no real thought, my eyes instinctively fall down to the children. It is just a natural reaction. No doubt about it, it is there with those little ones that moms and dads are either made or broken. I know that sometimes we just can't afford to keep our children in the latest fashions. In my house and among the children that attend my church, I try to deflate the value that they assign to name brand clothing. I consistently teach them to look for their value from within, not without. However, as parents we must keep in mind that peer pressure is a very strong force that our children have to contend with each and every day. Nobody wants to feel as if he doesn't fit in. For the part that we genuinely cannot afford to do, we must not worry about it. As long as we take pride in keeping them clean and neatly groomed, there will be a group of their peers who gladly will embrace them. God is so gracious. He is not asking us to do what we can't, but He is asking that we do what we can!

I know how hard it is to be there for our children when we ourselves are in emotional pain. After separation from my ex-husband, for all practical purposes, I was a single mom. There were many days when the stress and pressure of trying to care for two little ones was overwhelming. I felt as if I was continually pouring out of myself to the children emotionally; and, at the end of the day, there was no replenishment. There was no one there to comfort or encourage me. There was no one to make me feel that tomorrow would be a better day. Stacy and McKenzie were both so young, and they looked to me for everything. I remember the many times when the money ran short. The quarters set aside for laundry often had to be diverted for the more urgent needs. During those times, I would wash our clothing by hand on an old scrub board that my mom had given me. I would then hang them throughout the apartment to dry. I always ensured that the children were clean and well fed. I loved cooking, so they usually had a balanced, home-cooked meal set before them.

I wasn't perfect; in fact, I was far from it. Looking back, I see so many errors that I made. However, God was faithful. In a way that only He could do, He encouraged me to step up to the plate and be a mom to my children. Working in my conscience, He kept my responsibilities before me. When I fell off the deep end and could not be there for them emotionally, somehow God filled in for me and obviously ministered to my girls in ways that I may never know. I know that His presence was in that apartment and that He was actively at work. These two girls are now all grown up with families of their own. They never refer back to that time period as if it was challenging in any respect. Reflecting back, indeed they were very well balanced. There was no way that I could have provided for that, not in my emotional state. Truly it was God. I am so grateful because when I could not fulfill my purpose adequately, He came to my rescue. He would not allow me to fail.

If you are a mom or a dad and you have a similar story, know that just as God would not allow me to fail, neither will He allow you to fail. As He was there to pick me up, He will be there to do the same for you. Only commit your life and your ways to Him. He will get involved in every single aspect of your life. When God looks at you, He sees purpose, and your children are very much a part of that purpose. He has entrusted those precious little lives into your hands. He is allowing you to mold and shape them into vessels of honor. Do the very best you can to be a good parent. God will be there to see you through it.

WHEN GOD LOOKS AT YOU HE SEES . . . HIMSELF

Have you ever read the creation account as recorded in the book of Genesis? If you have not, take time right now to read and examine carefully the first two chapters of Genesis.

Every single thing that God created was spoken into existence with one exception—MAN. Man, His ultimate act of creativity, was His most prized and treasured possession. The entire world and all that exists within was brought forth and given shape by the power of God's spoken word. Yet, when He made man He did not speak; rather, with His hands He formed and with His breath He blew. From the dust of the earth, He formed man in His likeness and in His image. It is important that we pause here and note that these words *likeness* and *image* should not be interpreted at face value. Quite common in our culture, we would naturally assume them to apply to physical resemblance and stature. However, the Hebrew translation of God forming man in His likeness and in His image does not refer necessarily to physical qualities. More specifically, what is being addressed are the internal traits and character makeup of man. God formed in man the likeness of His own basic nature as it relates to intelligence, morality, integrity, and holiness. Into this molded clay, which housed like attributes of His nature, He gave life. He blew His breath and man became a living soul. From the very beginning God's hand was upon us, and His breath within us. Many try to ignore and to deny His existence, yet how can we escape the fact that it is His very breath that we breathe? It is on loan to us during our time here on earth, and when He summons for its return, life ceases. It is only because of Him that we live, move, and have being.

Perhaps you never have really given a lot of thought concerning the creation of man, but I am asking that you take a few minutes and just meditate on it. We literally were formed and meticulously shaped by God's very own hands. He placed within us His own basic nature. He then blew His breath into the molded workings of His hands and we became intelligible, spiritual beings. His presence is on us, in us, and all around us. It sustains, indwells, and empowers us. He literally touches every part of our existence. How can we not be creatures of great value? *(No matter what anyone is saying to you, no matter how cruel or how ugly, can you honestly deny your worth?)* We house the very spirit of God Himself. When He looks at us, He sees His image and His breath. We are products of His master design, the craftsmanship of His hands, and the breath of His spirit. Again I ask, how can we help but be creatures of exceeding great value?

During my lifetime, I have had opportunity to observe many lives transformed by the power of the precious Holy Spirit. Prisoners, drug addicts, sex addicts, and alcoholics—they were all labeled as social rejects, and no one really expected any good to come out of their lives. However, I personally have known and witnessed people out of each one of these groups who have had a life-changing encounter with the Lord, Jesus Christ. I knew their lives before Christ, and I had opportunity over a period of time to observe their transformation. They were new creatures; old things really had passed away and all things had become new (II Corinthians 5:17). Many of the very ones that society had counted out, today, they have awesome, thriving ministries, and their past is their most powerful witnessing tool. Wherever God's breath can be found, there is always hope, and there is always value. Although one may be lying in the gutters of life, if he is still breathing, it means that God is present. And if God is present, there is value—great value. God has a way of calling out to and connecting with His spirit (breath) inside of man; He knows how to communicate with His nature which resides within us. He can reach man down in the very core of his existence. Never are we lost or off limits to God. He always knows exactly where we are.

Please, you must know who you are. And even more importantly, you must know whose breath is inside of you sustaining your very life. Wherever there is anything that can be directly traced and identified as belonging to God, there is intrinsic value and worth beyond measure. When God looks at you, He sees portions of Himself. Think that through for a second. If he sees Himself in you, what do you suppose He thinks as it is related to value? God is not considering your value based on anything that you have or have not done. He doesn't see or judge your value based on who you are, who you aren't, where you've been, or where you've come from. As people, we judge all of those superficial type elements. However, God is not looking at nor is He concerned with any of our concerns. Pure and simple, you have great value to Him. It is His nature and His breath that is inside of you, and He knows the awesome and spectacular works that He can accomplish through you if only you would allow Him. It is not who you are or where you may be at this particular season in your life; rather, it is all about whom He can empower you to become. When He looks at you, He sees portions of Himself. And wherever He is present, the possibilities are absolutely endless.

Allow me to close this particular section with a little practical exercise. Bring the backside of your hand close to your mouth, leaving a little space in between the two. Now for a second or two just gently blow on your hand. Do you feel the stirring of air? Just know that the air you feel, which flowed from the inside of your being, it is the very breath of God. *As long as there is breath in your body—God's breath—no one can limit your worth unless, of course, they are attempting to limit God's worth.*

In the face of the enemy attempting to belittle you, without saying a word in your defense, simply raise your hand to your mouth and just gently blow. You have God's nature; you have God's breath. Allow the following two passages of scripture to minister to your inner spirit as they reveal God's awesome love for you. Commit as much as you can to memory, reflecting back upon it when you need it most.

You made all the delicate, inner parts of my body and knit me together in my mother's womb. Thank you for making me so wonderfully complex! Your workmanship is marvelous—and how well I know it. You watched me as I was being formed in utter seclusion, as I was woven together in the dark of the womb. You saw me before I was born. Everyday of my life was recorded in your book. Every moment was laid out before a single day had passed.

*How precious are your thoughts about me, O God! They are
innumerable! I can't even count them; they outnumber the
grains of sand! And when I wake up in the morning, you
are still with me! (Psalm 139:13-18 NLT)*

*"For I know the plans I have for you." declares the LORD,
"plans to prosper you and not to harm you, plans to give you
hope and a future. Then you will call upon me and come
and pray to me, and I will listen to you. You will seek me
and find me when you seek me with all your heart. I will
be found by you," declares the LORD, and will bring you
back from captivity. (Jeremiah 29:11-14(a) NIV)*

Prayer:

Father, when looking at me, You see purpose and You see Yourself.
Although the enemy often tries to convince me otherwise, I am
VALUABLE! Because of all that You have entrusted into my hands,
please help me not to betray Your trust. Without regard to personal
circumstances, I daily want to live out my ordained purpose in a manner
that always acknowledges and respects Your presence within me. Thank
You for believing in me. Amen.

Deeper Insights

*While we are spinning on our heels anxiously looking in every
direction for purpose, it is most often right before us. Every single
day of our existence is divinely packed and filled to capacity
with purpose; yet, this daily purpose is most often overlooked.*

While in prayer, I had allowed myself to become quite emotional.
I was conducting a revival, and I really wanted to do a good job.
It was a huge honor to be called back to my home church, and I
certainly did not want to let anyone down, especially those who had
selected me to be the guest revivalist. I wanted the meeting to be a

success. As I hysterically began to petition God for His anointing, asking Him to please, please bless the services, with a slight hint of reprimand, God responded that I had become too wrapped up in myself. The manner in which He was going to meet His people in the upcoming services and pour out His blessings upon them had very little to do with me; it was all about Him being glorified in the hearts and minds of those who would attend. Although I am a minister of the gospel and I want to be successful in what I have been called to do, God will not pour out His precious anointing just so that I might make a name for myself, impressing others with my "great" oratorical abilities. He revealed that His purpose for my life went so much deeper than being about me. I was not to be the awesome wonder on display that week . . . He was! All eyes had to be focused upon Him and Him alone.

In Ecclesiastes 12:13, we find our ultimate purpose, the reason that we have been put here on earth. King Solomon says that the divinely ordained purpose assigned to every man is simply to fear God and to keep His commandments. He said that this is the whole or the entire duty of man. To fear God and keep His commands, this is the ultimate purpose that we are challenged to carry out successfully every single day of our existence.

The way in which we communicate with others, the manner in which we conduct our business affairs, our willingness to help those in need, our commitment to promote the kingdom agenda freely and openly, even the way in which we handle our hurts and pains—God wills that our very manner of being be a compelling reveille call, summoning all to make haste and gather at His side. In the midst of personal trials, wounds, hurts, defeats, and yes, even in the face of sweltering abuse, as well as in triumphant victories and overwhelming successes, His presence must be clearly seen in our everyday living. We must be radiating beacons of light, graciously extending the only true message of hope. No matter our personal plight, that is still our purpose, and it is faithfully there to greet us each and every morning as we awaken.

I know sometimes we question how our disheveled lives could possibly bring any glory to God. However, the truth is that God's light shines brightest in the midst of extreme darkness. Consider Calvary. Out of much pain, suffering and darkness, the Father and the Son received immeasurable glory. And just as Jesus turned over the whole cross ordeal to His Father, we must commit our daily crosses to Him as well. It is not always for us to know exactly how He will manifest Himself to others through our lives, just be assured that as we commit our all to Him and rely on His unfaltering strength, He will cause His light to shine through us brilliantly.

As I pen these words to you, I am in the middle of a pretty severe physical battle. Multiple Sclerosis diagnoses hanging overhead, walking intensely labored, frequently stumbling and sometimes even falling—yet, through my everyday living I am charged to inspire hope, encourage faith, and make believers of all men. Through the gleam in my eyes and the glow of my countenance, the invitation must be extended to come and experience the Father's great love. Your purpose, my purpose, is to fear God and keep His commands at all times and in the midst of every situation. This is the whole of our assignment here on earth.

Chapter Five

Depression

*Y*ou want to do the laundry and cook for your family, but how? You hate *lying in bed all day, yet you can't seem to awaken long enough to respond to anyone or anything. Even the most menial tasks become monumental concerns. The glistening glimmer that once twirled and danced about in the children's eyes has been replaced with sadness as they silently watch you cry all day, everyday. As much as you hate that they have to witness you in that state, your emotions have long been outside of your ability to control. Unable to break your fall, with each passing moment, you plunge deeper and deeper into that awful abyss of gloom and sheer, utter blackness.*

While I am aware that hormone and chemical imbalances in the body can trigger depression, the disease itself seems to be fed and kept alive through the active thought life. For many, depression finds its inroads through some traumatic experience suffered or through severely troubling thoughts. Once entered into the mind, these negative images and thoughts just seem to grow in strength, number, and momentum. Taking on such a pervasive nature, it literally becomes impossible to shake free of them as they gain total control over the mind.

After the birth of my third child, Essence, I went through severe postpartum depression. Oh, the thoughts—they were all so very morbid and black. It has been over twenty years ago, yet I remember it all as if it were only yesterday. I felt as if another spirit had entered my being.

I did not know this new person nor did I particularly like her. There were recurring thoughts of suicide, and I worried that, in some type of uncontrollable rage, I would even lash out and bring physical harm upon innocent people, especially those living under the same roof as I. Often I would pray and plead with God that He would keep me from such unthinkable evils. As much as I desired, as much as I wept over the eeriness of it all, I could not shake the horrible thoughts. When I woke up each morning, no matter how early, they were there. When I fell asleep at night, still, they were there. They were even present in my dreams. I could not get away; there was no escape. I remember being tormented by the frequent nightmares. Heart wildly palpitating, startled and sorely confused, I often would jump straight up out of sleep. Even as I am trying to give you some sense of my encounter with depression, there are no words that can even remotely describe my experience. My husband was so very gentle, kind, and supportive. I knew that I could count on him. I shudder to think what would have been the outcome had he not been the loving and devoted husband and father that he was and has continued to be. I prayed a lot during that period. Indeed, God was faithful; He saw us through.

From that experience, I learned the incredible power of thoughts. They are an awesome creative force; yet, if not carefully controlled, they quickly can turn and readily become instruments of unimaginable destruction. Unbridled thoughts are the fuel that gives strength to depression. And when we first feel depression's onset, no matter how mild it may appear, that is the time to go to work, actively binding up all of those loosely flowing thoughts. The longer that they are allowed to have free reign, the more depression's grasp fortifies and the more entrenched we become in the ills of the disease. Experience has taught me the dangers of idleness, both physically and mentally. It is the idle mind that is most susceptible to entertaining the many negative messages that are presented to it. This is especially true if those negative thoughts have concealed themselves cleverly behind masks of consoling. While we all at some point desire some level of sympathy, know that what will often begin as a harmless pity party has the potential to mature and blossom into full, often chronic, depression. Be careful.

Many have had to endure much abuse during their lifetimes. They are left to bear the nasty scars of sexual, physical, and emotional wounding. No, it absolutely was not fair and the abuse never should have happened. However, in the face of all the pain and all the scars, you must use every ounce of strength available to wage an all out war against the spirit of depression. It desires to gain entrance into your being and bring a darkness so deep that, just as a person whose eyes have fully adjusted to the darkness, you eventually will lose all desire for light. A window shade suddenly raised, a door unexpectedly opened, a light switch flipped on—the very entrance of light will bring great pain.

You must oppose depression from every possible angle. Once it invades, it will be the epitome of all of your suffering, taking your pains and feelings of abandonment to levels you never knew possible. You thought it impossible to be in more pain than you currently are; you thought it impossible to feel more alone and empty inside. However, depression will heighten and escalate every pain and every hurt that you have ever experienced. *Please fight. You have already suffered enough. God will show you how. Don't give up hope. In due time, in His appointed season, He will deliver.*

Possibly the very best advice that I ever have received came through one of my former pastors. I can still hear the urgency in his voice as he warned, "Stephanie, guard your spirit. If you allow it to get off track, it will be hard to get it straightened out again." That advice has been most beneficial to me, and it yet stays before me. From the day that I first received it some 15 years ago, it has continually led me on a path of integrity and uprightness, governing many decisions that I have had to make. It is now very similar advice that I give to you. With utmost urgency, you must stand guard over your thoughts. While you are still in control of your emotions, you decide the thoughts that will be allowed to linger and those that will not. Using God's word, speak to your mind. Even if just one verse of scripture, speak it over and over as many times as necessary until the unhealthy thoughts finally take their leave. Refuse to dwell on insignificant matters. Although you may not be happy in your current situation, and perhaps it could be better, yet you must step away and analyze the total matter carefully, placing it in proper perspective. Is it a matter so serious that you are willing to sink into deep, drowning despair over? If you continue to dwell on your situation, slowly but certainly despair is going to creep in. And know that when it finally arrives, it will be so dark and so encompassing that you will feel powerless to tunnel your way out. Is it worth it? Some things . . . you must learn to release. God will help you; God will help us.

I literally believe that within God's word, there is an answer to every problem that we will ever encounter. Even if not summarized in a neat little package, guidance and instruction are definitely there. However, we must be willing to search them out. There are countless lessons in the bible from which we can glean. As I began to reflect on scriptures as related to depression, two particular passages came to mind. Allow me to share the essence of both.

The first passage of scripture, I Kings 19, tells of the great prophet, Elijah. In an open spectacle of triumph over the enemy, Elijah calls down fire from heaven. God responded and the fire fell. Imagine a man with that kind of favor on his life, that kind of connection with God. Now imagine such a man driven by fear as he runs and hides in a cave. There in his new hideout, we find him depressed and very distraught. He felt alone and abandoned, and probably he even had begun to question the meaning of his existence. Although obviously depressed, God still had need of him. After inquiring what he was doing in the cave, God then called him to come out. As the prophet came and stood at the cave opening, God caused His glorious presence to pass before him. Through His revealed presence and gentle whisper, Elijah's inner turmoil began to diminish, and he found renewed strength to rise up and carry out God's instructions.

Depression has a way of robbing us of our ability to enter into full, vibrant worship. We become somewhat oblivious to our surroundings, naturally as well as spiritually. Although God is always with us, the intensity of our pain and the deep emptiness that we feel inside cause our senses to become numb. No longer able to sense His nearness, we begin feeling that we are all alone and that there is no one who really cares or understands, including God. This is the very place where depression had taken Elijah. In the cave, isolated and cut off from fellowship and communion, God called out to him and asked, *"What are you doing here, Elijah?"* (I Kings 19:9 (b)). God wanted Elijah to take a step back and consider the real implications of his hiding out. Had he come upon a power that was greater than God's power to deliver? Is that what had led him to run? Although his life had been threatened, God was still omnipotent—possessing all power. Throughout eternity, there would never be a greater force—*not anywhere!* Elijah knew God's power, and he knew God's voice. He oft had experienced them both. However, fear and depression had driven Elijah into isolation; and, under the tremendous weight of it all, his knowledge of God had begun to wane slightly. Yet, God remained faithful. He refused to leave His servant there in that isolated place. When he seemingly could not find his way to God, God came to him. Causing Elijah to confess his fears verbally, there in the face of every tormenting evil, God caused His divine, calming presence to pass by. This passage of scripture does not record that after his encounter with God that the depression immediately departed. However, we do know that Elijah received the strength needed to leave his place of hiding so that he might complete the assignment that God had laid to his charge.

Just as Elijah was called out of the cave, God is calling you out of your place of hiding. Depression has driven you further into isolation than you really cared to go. Away from family, away from friends, and away from God—that is where it has taken you, and the return path now seems so very vague. Everything that was once familiar and commonplace—it is all concealed and hidden by the thick clouds of darkness. Although you feel abandoned and forsaken, you must take courage, knowing that God will not leave you in that place. He will cause His glorious presence to come upon you, and you will be endued with sufficiency of strength. God still has need of you; and, although you may feel it's impossible, you must force yourself out of hiding and move forward into His plans and purposes.

As you are regaining control over your emotions, it will be important that you keep yourself in environments that are highly charged with God's Spirit. (Attend worship services regularly and stay tuned in to Christian networks.) It is important to note that God did not actually enter the cave. Rather, He called for Elijah to come out. Forced to make a choice, he could stay inside his place of hiding, or he could heed the voice of God and come out. Choosing the latter, he moved to the cave opening, and it was there at that specific place that God manifested His presence. Even if Elijah was not instantaneously delivered from depression, at a minimum, we know that he was strengthened as he stood in God's presence. I believe that it is impossible for anyone or anything to come into direct contact with the awesome presence of God and remain in the same exact state. Contact with God absolutely works change, even if that change is not immediately visible. Following His self-disclosure, God sent the prophet back to work. Elijah did not leave the cave relying on his own personal strength. He stepped out relying on who God had just reaffirmed Himself to be. In that awesome, all-powerful strength that Elijah had just experienced, he knew that he had been strengthened, and he knew that he would be upheld.

The second passage of scripture that I want to share with you tells of King Saul and his battle against depression. Due to his continual disobedience, God allowed a distressing spirit to fall upon him. Greatly plagued and unable to find relief, King Saul was advised to seek out a craftsman, greatly skilled in playing the harp. It was believed that the soft, melodic tones would drive the distressing spirits away, granting the king the much needed mental relief. King Saul was very much in favor of the advice, and the search for a skilled harpist was to begin immediately. It appears that even before the advising council could leave the king's presence, memory jarred by what was obviously a most impressive encounter, one of the council members spoke up, saying: *"Look, I have seen a son of Jesse the Bethlehemite, who is skillful in playing, a mighty man of valor, a man of war, prudent in speech, and a handsome person; and the LORD is with him"* (I Samuel 16:18 (b)).

The man of whom the servant spoke was David, who would later sit upon the throne as king of Israel. What we cannot afford to overlook is the very last qualifier that was given concerning David: *". . . and the LORD is with him."* Israel had become the dread of many nations—many of which were mightier than herself—simply because of the awesome, all powerful God who fought her battles and ensured her victories. History had proven over and over that wherever Israel's God stretched forth His arm, success was already securely bound in the wings. This God whom Israel had come to know as an impregnable force was the same God who was mighty upon David. His anointing and His favor clearly could be seen resting upon him. When he put his hands to the harp, it became evident, even to the untrained ear, that there was something different, something very soothing and captivating about the light melodies that filled the air. Having secured David for the kingdom, when the distressing spirit would come upon Saul, David would simply play the harp. With great skill and precision, David's fingers would glide gently across the instrument's strings, creating such artistic beauty. God's anointing saturated the atmosphere, driving every distressing spirit far, far away. In the presence of God, there is renewed strength and there is peace.

I can't even begin to enumerate the many times that I have been consoled, encouraged, and uplifted through the very anointed music that flows from my daughter's room. If Essence is at home, you can count on her either to be singing or listening to gospel music. Either way, melodious melodies most often permeate the airwaves of our home. Many mornings awakened by the music, I will just lie in my bed totally captivated by the anointing. I dare not move. Entering into my ear, the music becomes a sweet, healing balm, flowing freely throughout my being, reaching down into the very depths of my soul and spirit. The tears gently fall as my bedroom is quickly transformed into a private sanctuary for two, just God and me. Drawn into worship, I joyfully enter in. Every thought, every concern, every worry, and every care—they all lift while in His glorious presence. In Him there is only light; darkness cannot stay. He pushes all the deep darkness in our lives far away.

When a close friend of mine was diagnosed with chronic depression, I tried to stay connected, as much as I could anyway. Many, many miles separated us. Whenever she began to weigh heavily upon my heart, I would phone. Before placing the call, I would petition God, asking that He would graciously allow His precious Holy Spirit and His anointing to be present and to be mighty through me. Many times she would be crying as she answered. I knew for sure that indeed it was God who had prompted me to call. Even through the phone there was such a dark presence, which clearly was detectable. It resonated in her voice, dominated her spirit, and it tormented her at will, giving her little to no rest. I would listen patiently as she managed to get out a few words in between sobs, offering advice when I felt it beneficial. In the depressed mind, sound reasoning becomes increasingly difficult as the many, non-ending thoughts begin to run together as one big inseparable mass. A friend who can be trusted to separate the issues, helping to bring light and clarity is to be highly treasured. That is what I really tried to do. I tried to reason through all that she shared and keep absolute truths before her. During our conversation, sometimes selecting passages from the book of Psalms, I would read softly from God's word. Like the great, calming quiet after a tumultuous storm, His word always ushers in such peace. She said that the reading always made her feel better, more peaceful. In my mind, that was a very good sign. Although her case was severe, there was still something in her which was open and responsive to God's word. I knew that her deliverance was sure; in due time it would be manifested.

> . . . and where the Spirit of the Lord is, there is liberty. (II Corinthians 3:17 (b))

Ministering to an increasing population of those suffering from chronic depression, there seems to be a common language used by many as they attempt to describe their feelings and their experiences: black darkness; a continual, non-ending fall into a bottomless pit; being mentally locked behind caged bars; hearing voices; uncontrollable sobbing; inability to get out of bed; and self-mutilation. Perhaps you also are familiar with this particular language, frequently using similar phrases to express your own emotional experiences. If so, there is good news that I must share with you. What you are going through, it is only for a season. In due time, if you will just hold on, God will deliver. I know that He will; I have observed Him do it in the past. Among my own personal friends that have suffered this condition—God was faithful. He delivered them all. In fact, the friend whom I referred to in the last paragraph has since started her own business (which appears to be doing quite well), and sounds happier than I have heard her in years. She sounds like the *in control, got a plan, working the plan* woman that I first met some fifteen years ago. Although chronically depressed, she never stopped attending church, faithfully placing herself in Spirit-filled environments. Many times through the tears, I have heard her confess that God would one day heal her. And God has done just that!

Please know that just as He has been faithful to many of my personal friends and to me, delivering us all from the tormenting spirit of depression, He will be faithful to you as well. I know that there seems to be no end in sight, yet at the appointed time, it shall pass. You can safely trust God to provide and to keep you safe during this very vulnerable period of your life. Even if it has to be in between long, gasping sobs—out of the depths of your very being, cry out to Him. Tell Him how you feel. There is no need for eloquent speech, nor do you need to feel ashamed and make apologies for your current state of being. Even though you are confused and feel very lost in the world that surrounds you, just know that He sees your exact location. He understands and knows how to interpret your cries and moans of distress. I give you my word—if you will only cry, He will answer.

Until now you have asked nothing in My name. Ask, and you will receive, that your joy may be full. (John 16:24)

Prayer:

Father, just as You have lifted others from the cruel grave of depression, I know that You will not leave me in this place. You are my hope; You are my deliverance. My soul waits and trusts in You only. I know You won't forget me. Amen.

Deeper Insights

Don't give up hope. In due time, in His appointed season,
God will deliver.

Over the past twelve years, I have been in some pretty intense weight battles. During those years I have had opportunity to sit back and observe eagerly as the unwanted weight melted and gave way to good old-fashioned discipline and exercise. Yet, much more often than I care to admit, I also have been forced to watch as the lost pounds found their way back to me. And of course, never did they return alone. They always managed to bring a few extra pounds along as well, soaring my weight to new heights. Having gone through many "lose one—gain two" cycles, I did manage to walk away with a very valuable lesson. I learned that whatever initial measures I had taken to shed the extra pounds, those same measures would be needed to keep the unwanted pounds from returning. Until there was a serious commitment to keep those measures in place, the battle would forever be ongoing.

As God brings deliverance into our lives, we can be sure that the enemy immediately goes to work to plan our fall. His desire is to re-enslave, bringing us back into the same bondage from which we have just been released. But just as deliverance is most often wrought through many tears, travailing prayers, and verbally declaring God's word over our situation—maintaining deliverance will require that those measures be continued. Once freed from the oppressing bondages, we must not abandon the intensity with which we seek God. Quite the contrary, we should cling to Him all the more. It is just the same as with losing weight. If the enemy is allowed to return, we can be assured that he will return with additional forces, making our latter state far worse than our first (Matthew 12:43-45).

Chapter Six

Birthing Samuel

I have always loved the biblical account of Hannah as found in First Samuel, Chapter One. Hannah had no children for she was barren. In desperation, she humbly petitioned God for a child—a male child. Finding favor in His sight, not only did Hannah conceive and give birth to a son, but this miracle baby that opened her barren womb grew up to become one of Israel's greatest and most revered priests, Samuel. Every time I read this story, I am reminded of my own somewhat similar experience. Well into the second month of pregnancy with my fourth child, I began to have some rather serious complications. After a series of varied tests, my doctor reported that I was in the midst of an artificial pregnancy and that there was no baby in my womb. He wanted me to undergo a certain medical procedure in hopes that it would stabilize my body, returning everything to normal. However, just like Hannah, for that child I prayed and I stood confident that God had heard and granted my petition. Standing firm in my faith, I refused the procedure. Needless to say, seven months following the doctor's report of an artificial pregnancy, my son, Samuel, was born weighing in at a whopping nine pounds, thirteen-and-a-half ounces.

Intensely meditating on Hannah's plight, God began to illuminate and open my understanding as it related to barrenness. He revealed that this humiliating condition went far beyond what most had ever really considered. Forever redefining this condition (for me anyway), He revealed that *barren,* in its truest sense, does not address the ability to give birth; rather, it directly speaks to the inability to conceive life. Conception, or more specifically the lack of, is at the heart of the matter. Simply stated, the barren womb is the womb that rejects all seeds bearing life, thereby making conception impossible. In light of this new revelation, I began to see barrenness all around me—not in the usual physical sense, but emotionally so. In the past when I would hear the term *barren*, I always limited it to a physical condition. However, barrenness goes far beyond that boundary, touching every single dimension of life—physical and emotional as well as spiritual. And barrenness in any one area is bound to impact the other areas as well. For the remainder of this chapter, as precisely as I can, I want to share the revelations that were revealed to me concerning emotional barrenness.

Ongoing emotional wounding, unattended scars and hurts of the past, the everyday reality of persisting pains and abuses—over a period of time these burdens become much too heavy to bear. With all resilience gone and no more strength with which to fight, those carrying these weighted burdens finally just surrender, succumbing to a state of emotional barrenness. There in an emotionally barren state, their ability to conceive or to envision that they have any value or worth is quickly lost. And although life-bearing seeds, which have the potential to build self-esteem, validate value, and affirm self-worth, present themselves, most often they are immediately rejected. Allow me to explain.

I shared with you in an earlier chapter concerning a young girl who was emotionally barren. I knew her personally, and I witnessed time after time as she consistently refused any and all positive compliments. These positive compliments were in fact precious, life-giving seeds. They had within them the power to build her self-esteem and help her develop a healthier self-view. Yet, if there was one thing that I could consistently count on her to do, it was to reject any and every compliment that came her way. When she looked at herself, she saw nothing of value, nothing of worth. And perhaps saddest of all, there was nothing in her that even remotely was willing to reach out and embrace that which could bring inward life. It was inconceivable to her that she might actually possess qualities deserving of special attention, recognition, or praise. Knowing that she had no sense of self-esteem, I made very conscious efforts to plant seeds of value within her, complimenting her often. However, every attempt was met with immediate failure. Before I could fully get the positive seeds from my lips, she quickly would grab them up and toss them to the scattering wind. If I commented to her that she looked nice, very quickly and sharply she would retort, "No I don't!" This was the scenario in every such instance. The utter shame of it all was that she really was such a beautiful young lady with a gentle, kind heart to match. Imagine a child not yet in her teen years already so damaged by life. Oh, how I wish it were only an invented illustration to help bring clarity, but sadly, it is a very real story.

Emotional barrenness devastates self-esteem as it strips away one's inner capacity to receive and embrace that which would bring about positive change and healing in their lives. It takes its victims to a place where they can no longer envision nor imagine that they have any value, worth, or potential. In fact, for the emotionally barren, it is much easier for them to grasp and believe negative self-concepts as opposed to that which is positive. Seldom is there any expectancy or anticipation for anything beyond the ordinary. And in cases where the ordinary is some form of ugly, ongoing abuse, generally there is no expectancy or hope for anything beyond the current abuse. All dreams of a brighter tomorrow have been swept away. Working a cruel devastation, emotional barrenness refuses to allow any form of life to take root. When that which potentially could produce life or generate hope is deposited, immediately it is rejected. The inner spirit of the emotionally barren has absolutely no tolerance for life-bearing seeds, quickly spewing them out as if they were a contaminated substance. Can you get a picture of how totally destructive this state can be? The horrible impact of emotional wounding and the utter depths of despair where it hurls its victims really is unimaginable by most. However, as dismal as this condition is, there is some good news: Even in barrenness, there is hope!

As we study Hannah's story, we find that she managed to lay hold on this hope. Acknowledging her condition, she turned to the only one who had the power to reverse her plight. Turning her energies toward God, Hannah goes into the temple and in quiet stillness utters her petition before Him, saying: *"O LORD Almighty, if you will only look upon your servant's misery and remember me, and not forget your servant but give her a son, then I will give him to the LORD for all the days of his life, and no razor will ever be used on his head"* (I Samuel 1:11 NIV).

Acknowledging our condition is the first step towards healing. No matter how or when we were wounded, we must truthfully admit our emotional condition, even if only to God and ourselves. Where do we stand? Are we in pain? Have we allowed our wounds to go unattended? Have they driven us into a state of barrenness, stripping from us the ability to conceive life? We may find that we are unprepared to answer such questions. Emotional pain does have a subtle way of deadening and numbing everything, even our ability to discern truths as they relate to our emotional health. Yet, it is still important that we self-analyze, willfully accepting truths as they surface. Wherever we find ourselves, it is from that very place that we must begin earnestly to cry out to God.

It was from a place of utter destitution and barrenness that Hannah began to petition God. She pleaded with Him to look on her misery. In His loving kindness, she asked that He would touch His maidservant and allow her to conceive. This also has to be our heart's cry before the Lord. We must ask Him to look on our misery in our current barren state. We must also ask Him to touch us that we might once again conceive life and that we might come to realize our great value. The only one who can work in our emotions and bring healing to all the broken, damaged, unfertile places is God. No one else has the power to do so. No one else can soothe the pains in our hearts and command the hurts to stop hurting. It is only God who has access to the inner sphere of man's existence. None but He can touch barrenness, commanding life to spring forth from that which has been dead long ago. Only He can enable us to move beyond yesterday's pains and passionately embrace tomorrow's potential. He alone is the answer. I meet so many wounded people, and it only takes a few minutes of being in their presence to sense that they are searching—searching for answers, for fulfillment, for contentment, for happiness, for approval, for affirmation. However, in all their searching, they fail to realize that God alone—not another mate—is the total fulfillment of all that they seek.

Now notice the latter part of Hannah's petition. She vowed that if God would just touch her womb, allowing her to bring forth a male child, she would then give that child back to the Lord to be used in His service. In fact, she promised that for as long as the child lived, throughout his entire life, he would be the Lord's servant. What exactly was Hannah saying? In essence, she was saying that if God would just give her the honor of conception, if He would touch the dead barrenness in her, then wholeheartedly she would surrender the fruit of that touch back to Him. All that she wanted was the ability to experience life growing within. She wanted to feel as the cold inner deadness gave way to vibrant life. Like sun parched ground yearning and thirsting for the gentle rain, she longed and ached for the ecstasy that only a life growing inside her womb could provide.

If we earnestly petition God to touch our barrenness, vowing to honor Him with the fruit of our conception, He will be faithful to touch us. However, as we are healed and made whole, we must not forget our vow. We must worship Him by offering back that which has been made possible only because of His touch. How often has God blessed His people to prosper, brought them out of bondages, and healed their sicknesses, only to have them soon forget what mighty things He has wrought in their lives? As God touches you enabling you to see your value, then you must reach back and help others to see their value. As He touches you to envision and imagine a better tomorrow, then you must take a message of hope to others, assuring them that there is something beyond what they currently see. Gaining the confidence to explore and put to use your many God-given talents and abilities, make sure that they are not used selfishly, benefiting only you. With these newly discovered talents and abilities, you must use them to bring praise and honor to God. And truthfully, the greatest praise that we can offer God is a surrendered life, dedicated to serving others.

Listen to this powerful statement that Jesus spoke to Peter: *"Simon, Simon! Indeed, Satan has asked for you, that he may sift you as wheat. But I have prayed for you, that your faith should not fail; and when you have returned to Me, strengthen your brethren" (Luke 22:31-32).* In no uncertain terms, Jesus was reminding Peter that once he himself had been strengthened, he had an absolute responsibility to reach back and help strengthen others. Again, with the fruit of God's touch in your life, you must use it to serve others.

I pray that you have been greatly ministered to through the pages of this book. This project has been very dear to my heart because it is my personal "Birthing Samuel" project. I vowed to God that if He would just touch me and allow me to conceive an instrument that would minister healing to the emotionally wounded, with the fruit of that touch, I promised that I would give it back, placing it in His service. I was so sincere in my petition, having no selfish or self-seeking desires. I only wanted to help sow seeds of value and worth into those who feel that they have no worth. I ached to provide relief; I wanted to help. Yet, I was barren in this matter, and I knew that I needed God to touch that barrenness that I might conceive a tool that He could use. Modeling Hannah's prayer, I asked God would He please just grant me the honor of conceiving and nurturing the seed. If only He would allow me to feel the growing life inside as He spoke revelation knowledge and healing truths through me—then that would be joy enough.

Now this is the miracle that you must know. There was a season in my life when I was much too broken to put my hands to a project such as this. In fact, I myself would have been among those most desperately in need of the healing that such a book could provide. During that time, I couldn't envision that I had any real talent. Never in my wildest dreams did I see myself as an author. What did I have of value to say? And even if I did have a message . . . actually to put it in book form . . . not likely! But somewhere in the midst of all my brokenness, God heard my inward cries of desperation. Please don't miss that. He heard my inward cries, the ones that I was much too weak to utter aloud and that were silently bottled up deep within. He heard the silence and He responded. Reaching out and touching me with His love, He caused the inside of me to come alive. He awakened talents, dreams, and desires within me that I didn't even know existed. Healing my brokenness and restoring my vision, He allowed me to see greatness beyond where I was currently standing. With the fruit of that healing, I now use it to serve Him.

God's promise to all who love Him is that He will never be further than a cry away. In fact, scripture reveals that even before we call on Him, He will answer (Isaiah 65:24). Think about that for a second. He hears our silent distresses, and He is responding even before we utter pleas for help. Fully set your heart on Him, knowing that He sees all of your hurts and wounds. He knows how hard it is for you to open up and trust another with your emotions. And not only does He see where you are, He knows the very experiences that have brought you to your current state. Yet, I plead with you, just as the physically blind totally trust in someone else's vision, when you can't see a brighter tomorrow for yourself, and you honestly can't see any value or worth within, then you must allow God's eyes to be your vision. Don't trust in your marred, blurred vision; trust in His vision, knowing that it is perfect. Your pain won't allow you to conceive a future for yourself, yet He sees the one that He conceived for you even before you were formed in your mother's womb. Draw close to Him and be willing to heed guidance, stepping into the path that He will direct. Although you can't see, trust Him to navigate the way, safely bringing you into a place of inner harvest. He will bring life to all those old, dead, barren places within. As you walk with Him, in due time He will touch you, enabling you to grab hold to life bearing seeds as they come your way. Your self-perception dramatically changed, no longer will you see yourself as one incapable of accomplishing. As new challenges and opportunities present themselves, flowing from deep within, you will clearly hear as your spirit begins to resonate, saying, *You can do it. You can do it. Really, you can.* When that long awaited day arrives, just be mindful not to forget the vow. With the glorious fruit of your conception, you must reach out and help others.

Prayer:

Father, I yield every barren part of me that refuses to conceive over to You. Touch the deadness in me that I might come to know the joys and fulfillment that inward life can bring. With the fruit of Your touch, I will go back and serve others. Amen.

Deeper Insights

In the past, when I would hear the term barren, I always limited it to a physical condition. However, barrenness goes far beyond that boundary, touching every single dimension of life—physical, emotional, as well as spiritual; and barrenness in any one area is bound to impact the other areas as well.

As my walking became more and more intensive and additional symptoms began to surface, I was forced to re-examine my convictions. I had always boldly confessed that God was sovereign and possessed all power, but now my confession was being put to the test. All that I had said down through the years, had those words truly taken root down in my heart? Exactly what was it that I had really conceived concerning the power that God possessed? Heaven forbid, but was I spiritually barren?

Those who are spiritually barren cannot conceive or fully believe in God's power. Although they may profess spiritual truths, deep down in their hearts there is no real capacity to embrace those truths. Then there are the emotionally barren, those who acknowledge and believe that God is all powerful; yet, they are unable to conceive that they are worthy of being touched by that power. So, on the one hand, there are the spiritually barren—those who are unable to conceive God's power. On the other hand, there are the emotionally barren—those who are unable to conceive that they are worthy of being touched by that power. On whatever side of the fence we may find ourselves, or perhaps even straddling both, the solution is the same. It is only the living word of

God which can lay open our hearts and cause it to conceive spiritual truths—the truth of who God is and the truth of our worthiness to be touched by Him. It is His implanted word which will reveal His great power and cause us to see ourselves the way that He sees us. Until the life-bearing seed, which is God's word, is accepted into our hearts, we will remain barren.

Chapter Seven

Starting From Here

Forgetting what is behind and straining toward what is ahead, I press on toward the goal to win the prize for which God has called me heavenward in Christ Jesus. (Philippians 3:13-14 NIV)

Chapters One, Two, Three, Four, Five—the creative juices were really flowing and I was definitely on a roll. Then, out of nowhere with no real warning, tragedy struck. In the midst of this project that you now hold in your hands, I lost my mom to pancreatic cancer. It was all so fast. There was no time to prepare myself emotionally or in any other manner.

When I arrived at the hospital in Lynchburg, Virginia, much to my surprise, Mom looked pretty good. Sitting up in bed talking with a life-long friend, a huge glow came over her as I entered the room. The next morning the doctors filled me in on Mom's condition. Due to the nature of pancreatic cancer, they gave her about six months to live. An only child, I had no brothers or sisters to help tend her; and, knowing that I soon had to get back to my husband and children, I made the decision to move Mom to Georgia with me. At least she could be near her dearly beloved grandchildren and me for the remainder of her days.

Arriving at a care facility in Georgia on a Friday evening, I spent the remainder of that day, as well as most of the next, getting Mom settled in. When Sunday finally arrived, my entire being, everything in me just shut down. I had no more strength remaining; it was all gone. For the past three weeks I had run non-stop back and forth to the hospital. There was also the emotional stress of trying to come to grips with Mom's condition, knowing that she was rapidly slipping away from me. And as if I needed another layer of stress, there was the difficulty of coordinating the move to Georgia. I had to find a suitable facility where she could receive the therapy that the doctors had ordered. Also, I had to contract a private ambulance service to transport her; and, because I knew she would not be returning, I had to close down her house in Lynchburg. Finally mustering the strength to crawl out of bed, it was around three o'clock Sunday evening when I finally arrived at the facility to check on Mom. I could tell she had been waiting on me, but in my heart I knew I was doing all that I could possibly do.

Mom seemingly had lost all tolerance for solid foods. During my visit with her, she asked if I would go out and get her some tomato soup. That seemed to be about the only thing that she was able to tolerate. Agreeing to her request, I left and returned with hot soup in a container ready to be served. I hung around only briefly after feeding her, heading home for what I hoped would be an evening of much needed rest. Around midnight I was notified that Mom had been rushed to the hospital. She was complaining of chest pains. Of course, I immediately assumed that it was nothing more than some sort of reaction to the rich, acidic composition of the soup. Almost immediately after eating, she had prepared for bed. As I was assisting her, helping her to get all settled in, it never occurred to me that it was not a good idea for her to lie down right after eating. Driving to the hospital, I resolved right then and there not to bring any other foods into the facility. It was just too dangerous.

The attending physician on call at the hospital found no problems with Mom's heart. However, because of her age, he thought it best to keep her a few days for observation. It was around three in the morning when, finally, she was taken up to a room for admittance. I followed closely behind as the attendants wheeled her bed through the long corridors. When we arrived at the room, the nurses began to get her all settled in. Everything was going along rather routinely when, all of a sudden, Mom just collapsed, slumping over in the chair where she was sitting. It all happened in an instant of time. Rushing by her side, I immediately observed that her mouth was twisted and that she had lost all use of her right side. Heart rate rapidly declining; long, labored breaths; staff and equipment flooding the room—it was all so very overwhelming. To this day I still can't come even close in describing the lifetime of emotions that welled up inside of me as I watched Mom battle for her very life.

The nurses were working very hard trying to stabilize Mom's vital functions. Seeing the sheer trauma that now covered her ashen face, I leaned over the bedside as closely as possible and held her hand; and, with as much melody as my streaming tears would allow, I began to chant the old, familiar Church of God in Christ tune—*"JESUS."* Over and over again I simply chanted the name, *Jesus*. Oh, there truly is something so powerful, so calming about that marvelous name. Mom was slipping away from me. Yet, in the midst of what should have been heart-wrenching, unbearable agony, the Holy Spirit engulfed that tiny, overcrowded room and transformed it into a sanctuary filled with worship.

I could sense the great calm that had come over Mom. Her inner spirit was at rest as she resolved to let go and release her fate into God's hands. Struggling to remove the oxygen mask from her face, she muttered apologies for errors she felt she made as I was growing up. In turn, I apologized for all the undue stress I had placed on her during my teen and young adult years. I then said, "No more guilt Mom. We will part knowing that we both love each other so very much. No more guilt." To that we both agreed. This time addressing Daniel and me together, once more through very muffled speech, she told us that she loved us both. I knew those would be the last words that I would ever hear my mom speak. We responded by telling her how much we loved her, and I then began sharing with her one of my favorite childhood memories.

Mom was a beautician. Often on her weekly day off, she would take me downtown and buy me a new dress. Despite my true tomboyish spirit, Mom really endeavored to keep me looking like a little princess. Generally our weekly outings would climax with an enormous lunch at Woolworth's Store. Sometimes we would sit in a booth, but my favorite times were when we sat at the counter. From there I could see the waitresses as they operated the big, old cash registers. I don't know why, but I was always so mesmerized as I watched them push the buttons on the register. I loved hearing the ringing sound made right as the cash drawer flew open. And then there were the turning counter stools. I still remember my dangling legs as I swirled around and around, stopping only long enough to take a sip of my thick, chocolate shake. Since it had been over forty years ago, I asked Mom if she still remembered our outings; she nodded her head signaling yes. Promising that I would not leave her, I stayed right by her bedside. I left only long enough to shower, return the rental car that I had driven to Lynchburg, and to check her out from the care facility where she was registered.

When my husband retired from the military, we decided to settle permanently in Georgia. In our minds it was the perfect location, being somewhat midway between his home in Florida and my home in Virginia. I usually made about two trips home a year, while he averaged only about one to his home. Probably because I had no other siblings, no matter how often I went home, Mom still wanted me to come more often. Over the years I carried a lot of guilt. The little girl in me still wanted to please her totally, and the price paid for not doing so was overwhelming, burdening down guilt. I felt that her expectations of me were often unfair. Her expectations versus my own personal desires—I often felt caught in the middle between the two, which ultimately created a bit of tension between us. Yet, for all of the tension felt, for all of the missed trips home, for all of the times when I failed to tell her how absolutely adorable to me she was and how deeply I loved her—for every missed opportunity, God allowed Mom and me to start again from where we were. In less than a minute of time, He enabled us to relive a lifetime, and all that happened in the past was forgiven.

When Mom first fell over in the chair—that could have been her final breath. Yet, God would not allow it to be so. He graciously allowed her another thirty-six hours. He knew that we both needed to clear the air between us; and if she didn't, I certainly did. Had that opportunity not been divinely provided, I really can't imagine how I could have ever come to peace after her death. So for that glorious thirty-six hours, I attentively held her hand, stroked her face, kissed her forehead, and told her how very much I loved her. Around two o'clock Tuesday afternoon, Mom's breathing became very faint and quiet. I knew the end had come. Knowing that I was alone in the room, the nurse on duty quietly slipped in to be with me. I appreciated her presence. Gently sitting on the bedside, she began to stroke Mom's right hand. I was on the other side of the bed holding Mom's other hand and gently stroking her head. I told her once again that I loved her and that I would see her in a little while. With a grace so characteristic of the classy lady that she was, ever so gently, Mom exhaled her last breath.

In the face of such tragedy, God was yet at work. To think that He loved Mom and me so much that even in the midst of death, He gave to us that one precious gift that only He could give—TIME! He so graciously allowed us thirty-six glorious hours that we might have opportunity to start again from where we were. Out of her death came beautiful, refreshing, healing life—healing for Mom, healing for me.

The message that I want to leave with you is simply this: Wherever you may find yourself at this particular season of your life, know that it is just that—*A Season*. It will not last forever, and it certainly will not be your end. You can go forward with your life. God is right there close beside you. He will not leave you, not even for a second, and He will be there to support and guide as you launch out and start again from where you are. When I think back to Mom and me, all along God had a plan so perfect for our healing. He wanted us whole. He wanted us to know that gentle, abiding peace that comes only as we totally forgive others and as we totally forgive ourselves. Over the years, I needlessly had built so many walls of defense—walls that now I am so very ashamed even to mention. After all, exactly whom was I defending myself against? Was it my mom—the one who loved me more than she loved life itself? Thank God that in a moment of time, He brought all those crazy walls crumbling to the ground.

Just as God had a plan for Mom and me, you must know that He also has one for you. You can pick up from where you are and begin again. Even if you are surrounded by a gloom and darkness so thick that you think it to be impenetrable, God is yet a master at commanding light to shine out of darkness. He will cause light, glorious healing light to shine upon you, driving away the dark hurts and pains. Like any good father, He desires to see you healed and happy. He desires that you be filled with confidence as you lean on His unfaltering strength. He will lead you safely to that new place where you get to start afresh. Trust God, knowing that He is committed to bringing you into your ordained purpose. Whatever hinders you from reaching your divine potential, He has a plan to deliver you safely from all those hindering forces.

All too well, I knew that my relationship with Mom needed some work. It had begun to grieve my spirit, somewhat affecting my spiritual walk. Yet, I felt powerless to do anything about it. I couldn't sit down face to face with her and communicate all that was bothering me. As much as I needed to—I just couldn't. But when I couldn't bring myself to make the necessary move toward mending our relationship, God intervened in a way that only He could have orchestrated. He placed the two of us right on the front line of battle. It was as if no one else was there, and we were totally dependent upon each other for survival. In that hospital room we were both battling for our very lives, and we each held something that the other needed—forgiveness. Mom sought forgiveness so that she could peacefully let go, and I sought forgiveness so that I could peacefully continue forward. Oh, how she absolutely loved me and I her, yet it was God who intervened and caused that love to flow freely between us as it should. God allowed us to start again from where we were.

For everything that is broken in your life that you know needs mending; for every tear that you have shed because the hurt was more than you could bear; for every missed opportunity to express love to those deserving; for every time you looked in the mirror and failed to see the great beauty and priceless value of God's creation—God has a plan to bring you into a new place. It is a place of abundant harvest. It is a place where the fields are lush and tall, gently swaying back and forth in the cool evening breeze. It is a place where the streams are clean and pure, offering sweet refreshing from the heat of toil. It is a place where all has been forgiven and reflections of the past have lost their tormenting terror. It is a place of new discoveries, new beginnings, and deeper understanding. It is a place that God has provided just for you. He provided it that you may pick up from where you are and graciously start again.

Prayer:

Father, since the beginning of time, You have been faithful to provide Your people with a way to start from where they were. No matter how entrenched we may become, never are we at a complete dead-end with no hope. I receive great hope and consolation in knowing that where I am in this season of my life, this is not my end. You have already prepared my place of turn around, a place where I get to start afresh and begin again from where I am. Amen.

Deeper Insights

Trust God knowing that He is committed to bringing you into your ordained purpose. Whatever hinders you from reaching your divine potential, He has a plan to safely deliver you from all those hindering forces.

I remember watching a television program where two men were stranded in the middle of desert country. What little food and water they had was quickly used up, forcing them to leave the campsite in search of help. One of the men, so weakened by the cruel desert conditions, was laid on a makeshift cot and physically pulled by the other. Unbeknown to the one pulling, somewhere along the journey, the man on the cot dies. Although quite delirious, as well as weakened by the burdensome load, the man pulling the cot just intently, almost in robotic fashion, continued forward, wobbling and staggering every step of the way. Now this is the irony of it all: The man pulling the load was weighted down by such a heavy burden—a burden that was dead and that should have been released long ago.

Sometimes we also are bearing the weight of a burden that long has been dead. Yesterday is gone. Knowing that there is absolutely nothing that can change or alter what already has occurred, we must find a way to release the associated hurts, pains, and bondages. Refusing to pull around *"a dead thing,"* we actively must seek how best to release it from our hands. Think about it for a second. Dead weight is the heaviest of all because it lacks the capacity to help support itself, leaving another to shoulder its entire load.

Many of the wounds that we carry are from childhood hurts. Whatever we have encountered—whether it be sexual abuse, grave emotional or physical abuse, abandonment, alcoholic parents—somehow we must find the strength and the wisdom to bury that which is dead. And know that if it is in the past, it is DEAD! However, it is the memories and the wounds that keep it alive in our emotions; and until those haunting memories and painful wounds are properly dealt with, we will continue to stagger and stumble under the weight of it all. It is so sad, but many of the burdens we bear are 20 and 30-year-old burdens. That is just much too long to pull around that which is dead.

Seek God. He will show you how to release every hurt, every wound, and every insecurity into His hands. He can touch you in the exact place of your hurt and cause healing to flow in an instant of time. Take comfort in knowing that for every dead situation that stands between you and your destiny, God will empower you to finally put it to rest, freeing you forever from its burdensome load.

Goodbye Insecurity

Goodbye insecurity
Goodbye despair
In my life you no longer reside
My eyes have been unblinded
Wounds have been healed
I can now see my beauty
It's about time I appreciate me

I realize my talent, my skill,
I'm uniquely, divinely designed
To carry out God's will
What a sigh of relief
To realize I have purpose
Only able to be carried out by me

This sad, salty water once poured out the ocean of my eyes,
It's now a refreshing creek that flows
Pure streams of joy and pride
Like an eagle I'll soar up,
Above and beyond
Flying higher for every fall
Each day becoming more strong

I'm a conqueror
My soul is a tree planted by the rippling streams
Gaining more knowledge from mistakes made
With my roots I soak up lessons learned and pursue my dreams

I can now raise my head with dignity
No longer am I ashamed, covering my face
Because I realize that its radiance
Makes the world a better place

I have so much to offer
That has the power to inspire
Lift higher—
My voice
My beauty
My hands
My spirit
My love
My smile
My femininity
How selfish of me to hide them
Because of puny insecurities
I'll show them wherever I go
Wearing each trait like an accessory
Letting them make my presence more glamorous

I'm illustrious
I'm the WO in *Wo*man
Full of confidence,
Not to be confused with cockiness
I'm simply one of God's chosen—
One of the best!

("Goodbye Insecurity" printed by permission of Author,
Essence Danielle Gant)

Other Books

By Stephanie Gant

Women of Destiny: Fulfilling God's Purpose

Issues: Healing For The Emotionally Wounded

Rizpah—Naked and Unashamed

For ordering information email:
sgantministries@bellsouth.net

Submit written requests to:
Mason Chapel Church of God in Christ
Attn: Stephanie Gant
1132 1/2 Roselle Street
Augusta, GA 30901

(706) 774-0030